THE
CAPACITY
TO SUCCEED

Fulfilling the Mission of Minority Business Development

Melvin J. Gravely II, Ph.D.

Edited by Barbara McNichol
Cover design and inside layout by Ad Graphics, Inc.
Internal graphics designed by Amy Winegardner

Printed in the United States of America.

Gravely, II, Melvin J.,
The Capacity to Succeed: Fulfilling the Mission of Minority Business Development
ISBN 978-0-9896204-0-6
Library of Congress Control Number: 2013944041

Mailing address:
Impact Group Publishers
P.O. Box 621170, Cincinnati, OH 45262-1170

CONTENTS

ACKNOWLEDGMENTS

I am always overwhelmed by the level of support I get from my family, friends, and colleagues. The base of my support is my family. They give me the room to do what I love. Thank you seems too little to say to my wife Chandra who has a unique and loving way of helping me stay focused on my goals. My three children Chereé, James, and Martin are equally supportive and encouraging. Thank you and I love you all very much.

I have written seven books over the years, but I have not written one in my own voice since the late '90s. The experience was enjoyable yet challenging. It took me a while to find and then to trust my voice. I owe a huge thank you to my editor, Barbara McNichol. She is always so positive and so clear with her input. Her experience was invaluable. Thank you.

The encouragement of my professional network kept me moving. I want to thank the loyal people who agreed to read and provide input to the manuscript well before it was ready for prime time. Thank you to Farad Ali, Pamela Coleman-Brailsford, Joan Fox, Angela Irby, Valerie Kimble, Arlene Koth, Rohena Miller, Cheryl Smith, Pete Strange, Rodney Swope, and Stanford Williams.

To Crystal German, who read the rough manuscript over and over again: Our hours of discussions about the concepts, ideas, and examples made this book what it is. I love the fact that you are always up to a meaningful debate. I appreciate the depth of your thinking and I appreciate you. Thank you. Again!

Of course, I cannot forget to thank Robin Bischoff. Thank you for handling all of the logistics of bringing this book to life and all of the little things you do every day.

To my friends at Messer Construction, thank you for your loyal partnership. This book is a testament to the way you have led the industry when it comes to enabling minority firms to grow their capacity to succeed. TriVersity Construction is just one of many examples of great companies you have helped develop. You deserve much more credit than you are willing to take.

PART I

What Got Us Here Won't Get Us There

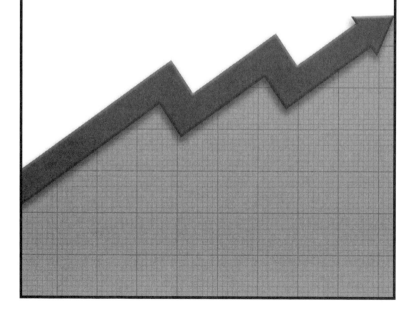

*Look at the signs
that things are different.
They're everywhere.*

CHAPTER 1

The Promise
Has Problems

John Wyatt felt honored. Stu Bails had invited him, along with two others, to what Stu called an "exit view." For almost 25 years, Stu had run a successful packaging company, and he'd become the most recognized minority business owner in the region. Now he was retiring, and John wondered how Stu felt about that.

Carol Street was another of the people invited. As Director of Supplier Diversity at Republic Corporation, she'd given Stu his first big break decades ago, and Republic had been his largest customer ever since. Carol had been an entrepreneur herself at one time, and now she'd earned a good reputation for working with minority suppliers.

The third invitee, Max Albert, ran a nonprofit minority business support organization called The Accelerator. Its mission was to *accelerate* the growth of minority businesses that had the capability to be suppliers to major buying organizations. Highly civic minded, Max was considered to be extremely successful by those who knew business. The sale of his valve manufacturing company years earlier had brought him significant wealth. Since then, no one in the area's business circles could think of any other sale of a minority business—successful or not.

John had owned his logistics business for only three years and, at age 36, was the "baby" in this group. Secretly, Stu was John's role model for success in business.

As John arrived promptly at 3:00, Stu's assistant escorted him into Stu's office. There, he found the others already seated around a small conference table. Over the years, John's access to Stu had grown, and he'd come to rely on Stu's advice. He'd been in this office many times. The room always appeared clean and tidy, and the worn furnishings with their outdated colors felt comforting. Around the walls hung plaques and memorabilia, many faded over the years from the light that poured in the windows.

As John came in, Stu rose to greet him, shaking his hand warmly. John hugged Carol as he always did and then shook hands with Max. John didn't know Max as well as he did both Stu and Carol, but he respected Max and his experience a great deal.

"John—how have you been?" Stu asked after they were all seated.

"Good, Stu. Thanks. But I can't hold a candle to *you*. Wow! Retirement. And from your own successful company! You've been *the* minority business icon around here for twenty plus years," John said, smiling broadly at his mentor.

Carol jumped in. "Stu, you know we're happy for you—even though I, for one, will miss our good relationship. Not only has your business with us grown over time, but we at Republic have learned from you how to be more inclusive."

"So tell us, Stu, how does it feel to be finishing on top?" Max asked.

Stu grinned gently, then his smile faded. "On top, Max? I'm sorry to say that's not how it feels. To be honest, it feels empty," replied Stu. "It feels really empty."

The others looked puzzled. "I don't understand," said John. "You've had a great run. Your business grew substantially, and you were able to employ a lot of people."

"And look at all this recognition," Carol added, pointing at the walls full of awards and mementos.

"You're clearly a wealthy man," said John, feeling perplexed. "You have what my peers and I all want. How can that feel empty to you?"

Stu responded with a slight chuckle. "When I hear you guys rattle off the list like that, my accomplishments do seem impressive. And don't misunderstand me. I'm grateful and I feel blessed. But still, it feels empty to me."

Stu leaned back in his chair, searching the ceiling as if to find his next words written there. "I know you consider all this to be the promise of success as a minority entrepreneur," he said, sweeping his hand around the room to acknowledge the items on the walls. "But I need to tell you . . . the promise has problems."

"Well, I'm struggling to see them," John replied, obviously confused by what he was hearing. "What are they?"

"The first problem," said Stu, "is that my business ends when I retire. And that situation is true for most of the minority businesses that came to market when mine did. The fact is, there aren't any buyers for a business like this one. Why? Because my value proposition is heavily tied to my minority certification. Only two customers account for ninety percent of my business, and my profit margins are half the standards for my industry. Even though I have a good team for managing contracts, my managers don't know how to grow a company."

Stu paused and looked around at his friends. "Max, you're the only minority business owner I know who grew a business and sold it. You know the national landscape in this regard. *Are* minority businesses being bought and sold out there?"

"Exceedingly few," Max admitted.

John jumped in. "Sounds as if you're saying you ran a bad business, Stu."

"No, I ran a *minority business,*" Stu replied. "No one gave us anything. We earned it, but we earned it because we could perform *based on our status as a minority business.* That's not enough anymore. Our relationships, sales strategy, the conferences we attended—everything—revolved around our status as a certified minority business."

"Stu, I am still confused. From what I can see, it worked. You made it," said John.

Stu smiled regretfully. "You're right. Everything you guys have said is true. I've made it so far—but now what? I'll likely have to close this business; then everything I've built over the last twenty-five years will come to an abrupt halt. The next generation will have to build again—from scratch. You call that progress? John, the programs for minority companies aren't sustainable if they're meant for only one generation to win. The game has to change."

"Stu, my peers and I see you as our profile for success," continued John. "Again, you grew a major business. You're a wealthy man. You've helped a lot of people. Everyone knows and respects you. That all sounds good to me. I understand it troubles you that your business hasn't 'changed the game,' but I like what it did for you—and I'm also okay with starting over from scratch to build mine the way you did."

"*That* is the second problem, John. You *can't*," said Stu shaking his head with a frown of concern. "You and your peers can't possibly repeat what my contemporaries and I have done. Not because you're incapable, but the world has changed. The marketplace is more competitive, and global sourcing has rewritten the books on supplying goods and services to large organizations. Carol, you know this better than any of us."

> The marketplace is more competitive, and global sourcing has rewritten the books on supplying goods and services to large organizations.

"You're right, Stu," Carol replied, nodding her head. "The process of doing business with major organizations has changed significantly, and it has nothing to do with whether or not the business has a minority owner. Think back twenty-five years. I was just joining the purchasing department then, and that function was much less sophisticated and much more locally controlled than it is now. Corporations were willing and able to make certain concessions for minority suppliers on points such as price and capacity. Now, we strategically source everything from raw materials to pencils. And remember when payment terms were, at worst, thirty days and could be even shorter if a supplier needed it? Well, our organization is executing a plan to move our suppliers from our current standard of forty-five days to seventy-five days for payment. Most of our corporate peers are already paying in sixty days. That means our suppliers will have to have even stronger financials and more access to capital to be able to do business with us. We certainly didn't institute this change to hurt minority businesses. We did it to become more competitive."

"The progress we've made in minority business development over the years also changes the landscape," added Max. "More sizable minority firms exist now than twenty-five years ago. This leaves less room for the new start-up minority firm offering a value proposition that's only *just as good* as the existing supplier. Why should customers risk changing from an existing supplier they know to a company they don't know that's merely offering the same value?"

Carol nodded. "Yes, if you add that to our internal desire to consolidate our base of suppliers in efforts to increase our efficiency, it all accentuates Stu's point. The game is indeed much different than it was decades ago. Growing a business the same way Stu did has gotten increasingly difficult and will only become more so."

"To complicate matters even further," added Stu, "when I started, the focus was on *minority firms* only. The term now is *diverse supplier*. Even if you wanted to do things exactly the way I did, you'd be competing with new groups of *diverse* suppliers, such as women, veterans, and GLBT."

Stu could tell John was struggling to wrap his mind around what they were saying. They were asking him to accept the demise of the vision of success he'd likely held for many years. It had to be tough to look a rich guy in the face and hear him say *you can't do what I've done.*

"Look at the signs that things are different. They're everywhere," Max observed. "But no one seems to be noticing. If they do notice, they aren't making any changes. It's like frogs in a pot of water being slowly heated to a boil. They feel it getting warmer and warmer, but they don't jump out. More and more, people are saying the big corporations don't care about supporting minority businesses. The truth? It's not that they don't care; it's that they care *differently.* They care based on their competitive needs and their company performance expectations."

"Guys . . . ," John said, holding up both hands as if he were pushing away their comments, "your picture of the future of minority-owned businesses is pretty bleak."

"Sorry about that," Stu replied apologetically. "It's not my intent to be depressing—and it's surely not why I invited you here today. In fact, I'm quite hopeful about the future of minority businesses. I recently invested a bunch of money in one that shows potential.

"John, we all think a lot of you. We see your promise, your passion, and your talent. You have what it takes to grow a successful enterprise. We're certain of it. Our intent is to realign your thinking according to our new understanding. The way we've done minority business in the past is obsolete, but we haven't changed and we have to. Trust me, there *is* a brighter future."

"I see!" said John, his worried look relaxing into a grin. "So this wasn't meant to be a celebration of your retirement but an intervention for me! Well, you have my attention. Sounds like I have a new model of success to learn."

Max looked surprised. "John, if it helps, I didn't know what this meeting was about either. Did you, Carol?"

She smiled and shook her head. "No, but I'm glad I came. I think I have some things to learn, too. And of course I'd like to help John in his endeavors if I can. Stu, why don't you start by telling us what you liked so much about the business you just invested in? What does it have that you find so promising?"

"That's easy," Stu said, reaching back to grab a book from his desk. He placed the book on the conference table and turned it so they all could read the title as he tapped the cover. "That company has what this author explains in this book. It has *the capacity to succeed.*"

CHAPTER 2

This Book is Not for Everyone

The Capacity to Succeed is about minority business capacity—defining it, building it, supporting it, and being rewarded because of it. Thus this book isn't for everyone.

Successful minority business development enables businesses to be "fully capable" to compete in today's competitive marketplace. I set the bar high on what *fully capable* means, and my definition goes far beyond the ability to effectively execute on contracts.

Minority businesses have proven over and over they can do that. To appreciate how I'm defining fully capable, imagine a time, possibly in the near future, when programs are no longer available to provide minority businesses with support and access to major buying organizations—a time beyond corporate spend goals and government procurement targets. At that time, what will it take for businesses owned by minorities to sustain themselves and prosper? The answer is the high bar of being *fully capable*. In the environment described, minority businesses must be able to obtain new customers, perform effectively, and make industry-standard profits, with all the business tentacles it takes to support these three capabilities.

Being fully capable has not been the focus of minority businesses in general, and therefore it has not been our outcome.

Look no further than the extremely low rate of merger and acquisition activity among minority firms. Firms with enduring value are acquired because they're worth buying. People want to merge with fully capable firms because of their attractive attributes. Fully capable businesses can create, sustain, and grow profits because of their value proposition, their business model, and their position in the supply chain. These businesses have been able to *leverage* their minority status without *leaning* on it.

Many minority business owners will quickly say they have this capability and may even be insulted by my assertion that many don't. Some may defend minority businesses and point out that many non-minority businesses aren't fully capable either. I agree—but this book isn't about non-minority businesses.

Other minority business owners and supporters are fine with the success they have right now. I appreciate how they feel and where they are. The minority business system has created opportunity for many of us to make more money and have more impact than we could have imagined in our youth. Still, others won't agree with my view of the future and therefore will see no need to change. I understand that, too, and respect their opinions.

This book also may not be for those corporate leaders who don't see their role as drivers of change in how success is measured in minority businesses. For some corporations, the "system" may not be broken, so they see no need for new thinking. They're comfortable with spend goals as their guiding metric and leave it to others to define the future.

Again, I can't argue with either minority business owners or corporate leaders who, after honestly evaluating their individual circumstances and futures, decide not to make any changes. We all have limited resources of time and money, and we're duty bound to invest those resources based on our priorities. That said, why should a major buying organization change? And why should a business owner who's created a level of personal wealth invest in changing? In these cases, maybe the answer is simply "they shouldn't."

> Over the last 20 to 25 years, the large, successful minority businesses were built on models difficult to duplicate today.

This book advocates for new thinking and different measures of success and for the need of minority business owners to face certain truths. The biggest of these truths is *what got us here won't get us there*. Over the last 20 to 25 years, the large, successful minority businesses were built on models difficult to duplicate today. They grew and prospered in a political and business climate that no longer exists. Now we have to embrace models for growing sustainable, prosperous minority businesses in our current hyper-competitive, global environment.

We can't logically deny that our business climate has changed and the way we approach minority business hasn't. The rules and roles and aspirations present for minority business in 1970 still exist today. So, yes, I am calling for those who are involved in the minority business environment to seek and establish a new way. I'm pushing an agenda of change and new aspiration. Why? Because evidence suggests that, increasingly, the business environment will put *more emphasis on the business capabilities* of minority businesses and *less on their minority status*. And not just emphasis on a minority business's ability to manage large contracts, but on all three of the elements presented in this book: the ability to obtain new customers, perform effectively, and make industry-standard profits.

Taken together, these abilities constitute *the capacity to succeed*.

Please consider the following important points before you read on.

1. *I am not judging what others want* from minority business development. Neither am I attempting to define success for others because I understand that various versions of success abound. Rather, my mission is to show the current reality, the opportunity, and a pathway to the future for a segment of minority businesses.

2. I believe the *future is bright for businesses owned by minorities.* I've met many minority entrepreneurs, and I feel their passion for success. The future holds the potential to provide a level playing field for minority businesses with respect to their non-minority counterparts.

3. This book is *based on research and observations* on what is working for minority businesses that are growing their capacity to succeed right now.

Pause for a moment and think about the political and business trends of the last 15 years. They include:

- supplier consolidation,
- global sourcing,
- the proliferation of race-neutral government programs,
- the redefinition of *minority* to include many diverse groups, and
- the increase in risk mitigation as a priority for customers.

Now think about how much the systems surrounding minority business have changed to address these new realities. If you're honest, you'll acknowledge they haven't changed much. Whether you believe in my view of the future or not, we're all assured of one thing: The future will be different from the past.

We've come far since the idea of economic participation was birthed by the federal government in 1969 (Executive Order 11458). To continue our progress, it's essential for all groups involved in the minority business system to play a role.

Major buying organizations have the most power and need to show they value firms that are building the capacity to succeed. Minority entrepreneurs need to think differently about how their Minority Business Enterprise (MBE) status supports their business. Finally, support organizations need to enable the new expectations and new definitions of success.

Who am I and What Gives Me the Right to Say This?

You might wonder, "Who is this guy pushing this strong message?"

Well, I can tell you I've seen minority business development and supplier diversity from all angles. Because of the variety and depth of my experiences, I've gained an objective understanding of the challenges, opportunities, and trends.

Further, my colleagues and I at the Institute for Entrepreneurial Thinking have advised the leaders of more than 20 major corporations on their approach to supplier diversity and minority business development. We've designed minority business development programs in communities across the nation and advised dozens more as they developed their strategies to grow minority businesses. In addition, we've evaluated 80 minority business support programs and worked directly with more than 100 minority entrepreneurs to help them grow their capacity. This interaction has substantially added to our knowledge and understanding of the issues.

I've personally run seven different companies in seven different industries. I've started businesses from scratch and acquired them, too—both with business partners and solo. My businesses have achieved sales from $16K to $60 million, with many levels in between.

For the last five years, I've focused my research and development on the idea of building business capacity. Everything I've come to know leads to one conclusion: The path to future success will be based on activities and expectations much different from those in the past.

I've discovered—and present here—the dynamics behind creating a holistic capacity that drives business success.

Sound intriguing? I invite you to read on if you'd like to know more.

PART II

We Don't Understand Capacity

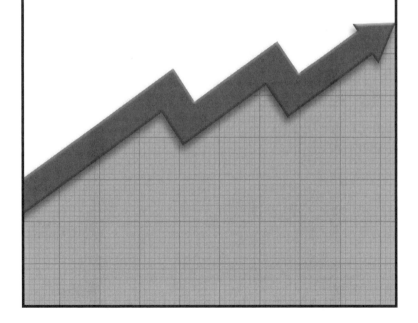

*The goal is not
to be big; the goal is
to be successful.*

CHAPTER 3

Re-Defining Capacity

What's the difference between a firm with capacity, or size, and one with the capacity to succeed? To be honest, far too few minority firms have either, but even in the rare occasion when a firm grows what we call capacity, its size alone doesn't make it successful. We measure size in a number of ways, including level of sales, number of employees, and number of locations. Size, however it's measured, has been our proxy for capacity.

Let's say a business has $900 million in sales and 3,700 employees. Does it have capacity? Sure it does. But what if it has only one customer and, because of its relationship with a majority company, it achieves only 20 percent of the profit margin of its industry peers? This, by the way, is a true example. The company does have one of the elements of the capacity to succeed, which is significant size and related volume of work. However, to be fully capable in today's world, the business needs the other two critical elements: the capability to 1) get more customers and 2) generate industry-average profitability.

The idea of the *capacity to succeed* comes alive when you unpack it. It's the business's capabilities to get work, do work, and get paid. These are the three general capabilities that allow a business to sustain itself and prosper in its particular industry. Every successful company must have these three, and none is

23

The Capacity to Succeed

Figure 3.1. The Three Elements of the Capacity to Succeed

more important than another. Great organizations find their comfortable balance among the three. Don't be fooled. Being big is not enough.

Size is Important, But . . .

Having a sizable business is sexy. I get it. All things being equal, I'd rather have a large company than a small one. And size can be helpful, especially when it translates into the elements needed to get more customers, keep them happy, and make more money.

In addition, size can enable a business to have more assets such as resources, expertise, and geographic reach. It can also mitigate risk or in some way drive additional value to the customer. But even then, size alone is not the final word on capacity. The goal is not to be big; the goal is to be successful.

That means having increasing numbers of satisfied customers with whom you're able to make industry-standard profit. Getting contracts can make you big, but they don't always make you successful.

It's What You Can Do That Counts

Customers want a business that can fulfill their needs, depending on the interaction. If they can't get a return telephone call, they want the company to be more responsive. If a proposal is late or poorly done, customers want the company to pay more attention to detail. If the pricing is too high, they want the company to do what's necessary to lower price, such as invest more in technology, process improvement, and driving economies of scale. We talk about size, but customers care more about the business's *capability* to meet their needs than size.

The capacity to succeed focuses on what a firm can *do* and less on what it *has* in terms of sales and employees. It thus translates into a broad view of what a firm is capable of doing.

More and more business leaders are talking about building capacity these days. They either claim to be doing it, ask for it to be done for them, or wish they could figure out how to do it. Yet today, there's neither any definition of capacity building nor any means to measure whether it's actually happening.

Do We Really Want What We Say We Want?

A friend asked me, "What if spend goals and special programs are all corporations and minority business owners want? They aren't all that bad, and they allow corporations to tout their successes in minority business spending.

Minority business owners make money and maybe even create personal wealth."

I offer two truths in answer to this question. First, these goals and programs may be all people want because it's all they know when it comes to minority business "success." Second, the dynamics of politics, culture, and, most of all, business have changed. The thinking, activities, and metrics for success that got minority businesses to this point won't work going forward.

What Got Us Here Won't Get Us There

No doubt, minority programs have provided opportunity, grown businesses, and created diverse wealth. But the market demands the minority business industry move faster and further to provide a rational return on investment and project sustainable growth into the future. Market dynamics have changed, but our approach to minority business development hasn't, so we're already experiencing diminishing returns on our minority business efforts. And this situation is likely to get worse.

> The minority business system is a way of being in business but not a means to grow a business.

What's the core problem? The minority business system is a way of *being in* business but not a means to grow a business. The system isn't designed so participants can leverage the programs to achieve success; rather, it keeps us needing the programs in perpetuity to stay in business. Investing in the *capacity to* succeed becomes the long—and therefore often discarded—route.

Current minority business rules don't provide incentive for building the capacity to succeed, so even well-intentioned business owners who may be strapped for resources and hungry for opportunity do what makes sense under the circumstances. They seek the lowest and easiest point of entry—the one that drives the most spend and presents the least amount of personal risk. Not, typically, the best business.

Such a system doesn't drive us toward the types of business strategies we say we want and those the market clearly demands.

Rather, the current competitive landscape demands minority business efforts create more value, be better aligned with market trends (globalization, risk management, supply chain leverage, etc.) and create a better model of sustainability. None of our current metrics recognize, reward, or even define this path. Instead, they're focused on providing access and achieving spend goals.

Progress Rests on One Key Question

More important than anything mentioned is the answer to the question, "Are we willing?" We keep talking our way past the challenges that demand real action, but the capacity to succeed demands we *change* in a number of areas. The rest of this book explores the needed changes and how we can make them. But face it. No book can make us a willing participant in change.

For some, the "success" they currently have will amount to all they want. Others won't see the threat of using old models and will also choose a different path. Still others will hide behind saying, "We *want* to build capacity, but we don't know how." What they really mean is, "We're not willing to do all of that, so show us an easier way that demands less change on our part—a way with a lower investment and, of course, a way that gets us there in less time."

Although good dialogue is taking place about capacity building, we're still clinging to old myths about how capacity is built—which the next chapter aims to dispel.

CHAPTER 4

Myths About What Builds Capacity

Until now, no one has specifically defined capacity and what it means to build it, which may be why it was not being built in minority businesses.

Capacity is directly related to a business's capability to do something in the marketplace. Therefore, building capacity means *engaging in activities or experiences that create additional capabilities so a business can do something more than it could before.*

Because of myths that misrepresent the concept and confuse the issue, most activities billed as capacity building can't pass the test. Let's look at a few of these myths.

Myth #1: Increasing awareness builds capacity.

Few of the activities major buyers and support organizations promote under the banner of capacity building do the job. For example:

- Four-hour training programs on marketing
- Most mentoring programs
- Week-long executive management programs
- Sessions for understanding LEED, LEAN, and Six Sigma

Trust me, I've attended them all and even conducted some. They're *not* capacity building. The executive education courses that focus specifically on minority businesses are outstanding sessions that involve a significant investment of both time and money. Taught by enlightening and engaging professors, these courses present topics relevant to the needs of the business leaders. They're not perfect, but they *are* first-rate.

So why don't these sessions build capacity? The answer is the subtle but significant difference between *knowing about* something and being *able to do* something. Most activities called *capacity* building are better described as *awareness* building.

> Most activities called capacity building are better described as awareness building.

To be sure, awareness is often the first step to capacity building. It means a business leader or owner was exposed to new ideas and concepts and perhaps came away with new insights. However, the fact that leaders now *know* these ideas doesn't mean their business can put them into *action* and *do* what's required to add another level of capacity.

The same thing can be said about coaching, mentoring, and business roundtables. They're valuable when done well, but in effect, they build awareness, not capacity. You can feel the frustration in the people investing in, developing, and deploying these awareness-building experiences. They can't understand why all this education doesn't translate into more capacity. And the truth is, it never will.

Myth #2: Big opportunities grow capacity in small firms.

Most of the time, small firms don't play a significantly strategic role regarding large opportunities. The small firm may invest in the temporary "capacity" required to do the work and meet the needs of the project. But business owners know big projects come to an end. What do they do? Add resources that need little investment and can be shed quickly because getting big projects is rare. Who knows when the next one will come along?

These investments typically don't add to the capacity to succeed. The outcome is a sizeable rollercoaster ride that, for most firms, ends with a capacity equal to where they started. Of course, large opportunities offer benefits for small firms: The firms can add the notable project to their experience, and the revenue from these projects does drive cash flow and profit. That said, although they're high profile, major projects rarely add to the capacity to succeed. They're not nearly the tool to grow capacity they're advertised to be.

Myth #3: You can grow the capacity to succeed in spite of the business owner.

No one wants to say it aloud. Maybe no one sees it. But it's true: You can't grow a firm's capacity to succeed without the active, intentional, and capable participation of the business owner.

People fall in love with the potential of a business or with the personality of the owner. Neither matters, though, if the business owner isn't committed and able to build capacity. Many factors contribute to whether a firm can build the capacity to succeed, but everything starts and potentially ends with what the business owner *wants*.

When I say "wants," I don't mean what he or she would *like* to have. I mean what the owner is willing to invest in, plan and learn for, delay gratification to have, and persevere to do.

Unfortunately, we can't only listen to what business owners say; they've been trained to say what they *ought* to want. It's no different than people working in a job. They *ought* to want to be promoted to the next level; they *ought* to want to manage people and take on more responsibility. So even if they *don't* want these things, they think they ought to *say* they do.

Business owners are in the same situation. They say they want to grow bigger, get larger contracts, and expand their geographic reach, even if they don't actually want to—*because they secretly fear their businesses will die if they don't*. Or maybe they really *do* think that's what they want—until they begin to understand what it takes. Are they willing to risk their house, retirement money, and financial future? Are they willing to make less money than the people who work for them as the business grows? Those who've had to face these questions know what I mean. It's not easy to honestly say "yes" to growing capacity.

To be sure, having a business with capacity is cool. The business wins awards and gets media attention, and its success upgrades the owner's lifestyle. But the process of getting there isn't as pretty as the final picture. Business owners have a lot to consider if they truly want to grow the type of organization that can break from the constraints typically holding back minority firms. Before enjoying the success business owners say they want comes the necessary sacrifices and tradeoffs.

So if you're involved with a company and would like to build its capacity, get clear about what the owner *really* wants. Make sure it's not merely what he or she would *like* to have. Know that everyone involved will be sorry if owners are pushed to be in business in a way they don't want to be—like trying to milk a bull. You'll waste a lot of time, become frustrated, get no milk, and annoy the heck out of the bull!

To reiterate, activities such as education, mentoring, participation in large opportunities, and inviting the business owner's involvement are important, but you can't stop there and expect capacity to build automatically. It won't. As you'll see going forward, the capacity to succeed is *bigger* and *deeper* than a class or workshop could possibly be. Building the kind of capacity needed for a fully enabled firm to compete in today's hyper-competitive market takes time and ongoing attention.

*Tremendous
financial and emotional
investments have been made
in building the current system.*

CHAPTER 5

Distracted by the "Rules" of Minority Business

This chapter could be seen as directed only to major buying organizations. It's not. The subject concerns *everyone* involved in the minority business industry. Each person can benefit by understanding how the minority business system drives our behavior, creates opportunity, and provides incentive to our business strategy as well as the strategies of others in the supply chain.

I want you to know I "get" it. I know why things are the way they are. I know why people think as they do about the norms of minority business such as spending goals, best practices for major corporations, and limits on net worth as a means to be certified. Every industry needs standards, a means to track progress, and a method to report on results. All of the standards make sense—*if* you don't consider their impact on building the capacity to succeed.

The spend goal is a great example.

Should the Spend Goal be the Most Important Metric?

Whether a buying organization reports its spend goal using a dollar amount or a percentage of its total spend, the spend goal is the gold standard for evaluating the success of supplier diversity. Relatively easy to determine, it's close to an "apples to apples" comparison among major buyers and easy to report to external stakeholders. It works.

However, a spend goal also incents (and maybe even promotes) behaviors that can potentially kill capacity, such as pass-through transactions (business transactions that get billed through the minority supplier but that are *passed through* to be executed by a non-minority business).

Another example of how spend goals can be a dis-incentive to capacity-building behaviors is the focus on high-dollar supply-chain categories such as fuel, computer hardware, and construction. The bigger the dollar volume, the easier it is to reach what are often lofty spend goals. But the focus on high-dollar volume doesn't incent innovative solutions, nor does it open opportunities in areas of less spending such as professional services (legal services, architecture, marketing, etc.). Minority/majority joint ventures with the sole value proposition of driving up minority spend are an additional example of how spend goal targets can motivate activities that don't support a market-oriented, growing business for the minority owner. (See Chapter 15 for more on how to evaluate an effective minority/majority relationship.)

Best Practices for What Outcomes?

Best practices add value because they set a threshold of expectations and can help one corporation learn from another. They affirm, "Hey, this is what commitment looks like." In short, they work. The question is, what are they working *toward*?

We say we want capacity growth in minority firms. But do our best practices support it? In truth, a number of "best practices" have nothing to do with building capacity—yet they become the focus of most supplier diversity efforts. For example, best practices might include:

- How a firm tracks data
- How supplier diversity is staffed
- Where supplier diversity reports in the organization (purchasing, HR, community development, sales, etc.)
- Whether a type of spend can be counted as direct or indirect
- Whether a solution resides tier one or tier two

These are process issues, not outcomes. The industry spends more time talking about these issues than they do about building capacity.

So what if a corporation has no supplier diversity department and no system to track its tier two spending, nor a special web portal for minority businesses? Yet, it works with 10 minority suppliers to improve the suppliers' capacity to supply to them (as well as succeed with other major buying organizations). What if the minority suppliers with whom this corporation works grow in size, capability, and strength? Isn't that the point? The minority business industry would rate this corporation as a failure if it used best practices as the measure.

> Best practices and spending targets are powerful tools right up to the moment they become the actual end goals.

Best practices and spending targets are powerful tools right up to the moment they become the actual end goals. If we

want to have minority suppliers that have the capacity to succeed, then we must declare that outcome as our end goal.

Certified Not to Grow Wealth

Certification is a valid best practice. Certifying that a firm is truly owned and operated by a member of a recognized minority
group is critical to the integrity of any minority business effort.
But the idea, through either policy or practice, that a minority
firm must be poor is ridiculous. The most obvious examples of
this issue of wealth are government agencies that have a certification policy limiting how much net worth an owner can have
and still be certified. It just doesn't make sense. What message is
this giving to minority entrepreneurs? "I want to work with you
until you actually grow the capacity you need to serve me best,
and when you begin to accumulate wealth as a benefit of your investment, I'm no longer interested." For many, the term *minority*
has become synonymous with poor, struggling, and unprepared.

Most of the players in the minority business industry are
afraid to talk about wealth creation. But how can we talk about
building the capacity to succeed without expecting business
owners to grow wealth? Wealth is a desired outcome of entrepreneurship, and it's not beneficial to assign a lower standard
for minority businesses.

For good reason, the minority business industry struggles
with this concept. Outside of the government policies, most
of the signs of the struggle with wealth creation are subtle.
Someone might say something as harmless as "that company
has gotten big enough. Let's help someone else." Or "why does
that company get all the business?" Well, maybe it's because
that company is the best; it's making the right investments in
its capacity to succeed.

I understand the idea. Don't help people unless they need the help. But that doesn't lead to growth in capacity and positive economic development outcomes. Plus, the limiting factors on minority businesses go far beyond financial. In fact, finances might be the least limiting factor for most. Minority businesses experience social limitations, relationship limitations, legacy limitations, and—the strongest of all—limitations based on how minority businesses are perceived in the market place.

Part of this negative perception is rooted in how minority programs have been oriented.

A Social Orientation is Limiting

It's common to think about helping those in the most need, not necessarily those most capable of using the help. But this social paradigm doesn't lend itself to growing substantial minority businesses.

It's difficult, if not impossible, for nonprofit support organizations or government agencies to obtain funding for an initiative designed to help individuals grow wealth. So minority support organizations seeking funding present the "social value" proposition instead.

Truth is, *wealth* is what we really want. Wealth creation is the outcome of business success, and business success means we've built a business capable of serving customers. Plus, wealth-creating businesses hire people, invest in communities, and participate in philanthropy (delivering more social value). On average, minorities are more prone to give than whites. In some cases, they give up to 25 percent more, according to "Cultures of Giving," a report by W. K. Kellogg Foundation (January 2012).

Yet, wealth is rarely mentioned in the minority business industry. We do want professionals who have worked for corporate America, even if they've accumulated personal wealth. We want them because they've also gained valuable knowledge and experiences that could help them grow a business with the capacity to succeed. We also want to continue to enable existing minority business owners who have grown their business over the years and, in the process, have accumulated some level of wealth.

Why do we want them? Because they intend to add value, take risks, and continue to grow their business. I say this assuming the capacity to succeed is our goal. But yes, I also hope they grow more wealth. That's the idea.

Respect the Rules, Focus on the Goal

This cold fact remains: *Much of the support designed to provide access for minority firms and hold organizations publicly accountable can distract us from doing what we need to do to build minority firms with the capacity to succeed.*

I hold no illusions that my rants will actually get people to change. That would be like expecting real changes to our income tax system. Such change is tough to effect because of the entrenched infrastructure of organizations, businesses, and interests that keep the system as it is. Likewise with the minority business system. Tremendous financial and emotional investments have been made in building the current system. If I were king for a day, I would change a few things; but in lieu of my coronation, I suggest we add activities, expectations, and metrics that support growth in our capacity to succeed.

Major buying organizations aren't the only ones that get distracted by the rules. In fact, everyone does. I've seen majority companies allocate a project's work in such a way that made no logical sense and even hurt the project. Why did they separate the work the way they did? Because a portion was exactly 15 percent—the goal for minority participation. They got distracted.

I've witnessed debates about the "proper" way to count tier-two spend and how it rolls up into the overall spend goal. These people got distracted. I've seen minority business owners approach major buying organizations and announce they were there to help them reach their minority spending goals. If minority status was the only value they offered, they were also distracted. Indeed, it's easy for everyone involved to become distracted by the industry rules.

When in doubt, ask this question: "Do these issues matter to developing firms with the capacity to succeed?" Your answer should help you refocus. Respect the rules, but focus on the goal.

...businesses win or lose in the marketplace based on how well they execute the core components...

PART III

Building the Capacity to Succeed

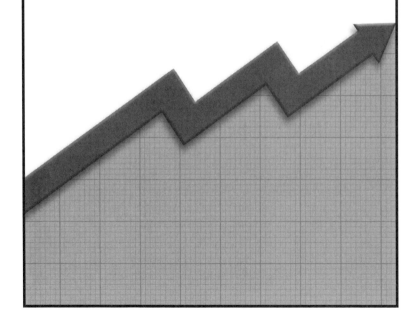

... a firm can make horizontal investments forever and never reach a point of sustainability...

CHAPTER 6

Investing in the Capacity to Succeed

A real conversation about capacity building isn't possible without including serious talk about investing because *investments enable the building of capacity.*

An investment means committing resources now and expecting a return or benefit in the future. Because the returns are realized later, they're uncertain. Investments often require delaying gratification, deferring consumption, or tying up a resource that could be used for other things—all in the belief that a future gain is worth the tradeoff. Every day, businesses decide to invest or not, and they decide based on the following realities:

- How much a business owner believes in the return, i.e., believes that the investment will lead to more opportunity; that it's the only way (or at least the best way) to reach a particular objective; that the return can be expected fairly soon. (The sooner the return, the easier the decision.)
- How much in the way of resources (money, time, energy, etc.) the owner has available to invest.
- How successful previous investments by the owner have been.
- What the owner's investment alternatives are.

- How clear the owner is about what he or she really wants.

- How clear the owner is about what the "right" investments are to get what he or she wants.

The more resources, experience, and clarity business owners have, the more comfortable they are investing in general and investing specifically in building the capacity to succeed. But if they don't believe in the future, or if they believe they can reach their objectives without investing, they don't invest. Who can blame them? That's why it's so important for the minority business system to recognize and encourage business owners who are investing in building their own capacity.

Not All Investments are Equal, but They All Matter

"Investments" made in resources to meet the needs of a particular opportunity are the easiest investments to make. For example, a business wins a contract to repackage four individual containers of shampoo into one shrink-wrapped package so it can be sold as a single unit. The business increases its labor force by 20 percent to process the order and rents 20 percent more plant space to accommodate the additional workforce. The business has increased the amount of work it can do—what we typically think of as its capacity. That's good. As a result, more people have jobs, new space is occupied, and the owner reaps the benefit of the profit generated.

HORIZONTAL INVESTMENTS

The investments the business put forth in this example are *horizontal investments* tied to a specific revenue stream. Typically, horizontal investments are those involving more people, more raw materials, and other resources that add to how much work a business can do. These types of investments are easy to make because they're tied to a known return that's near-term. The business owner *believes* the specific opportunity is real and the business will be paid in a timely manner.

However, making *only* horizontal investments is limiting. Consider the four quadrants shown in Figure 6.1. Horizontal investments can increase the size of an organization but still leave the company limited in its capability. A horizontal investment can move the company from quadrant one (constrained) to quadrant two (larger but limited). Quadrant two is a better position than quadrant one, but the firm still isn't fully capable. Horizontal investments add to how much a business can do, but they do little to add to a firm's capability to get more work or improve profitability from the work it does.

Horizontal and Vertical Investments

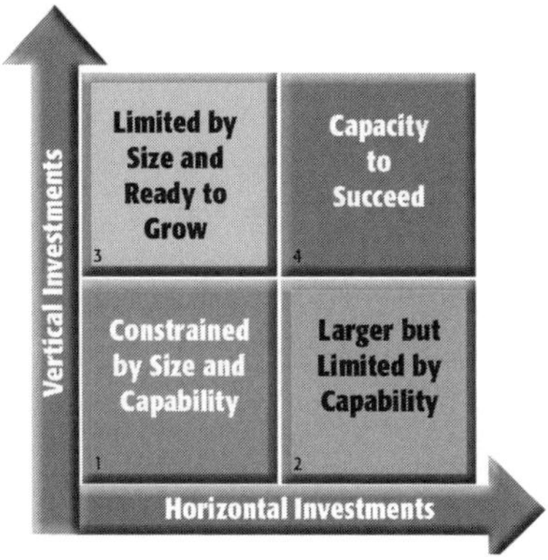

Figure 6.1. Horizontal and Vertical Investments

VERTICAL INVESTMENTS

Vertical investments are called this because they move a business "up" in the areas that can complete the capacity to succeed. They move a firm up into quadrant three (ready to grow) and position them for the desired quadrant four (the capacity to succeed). Vertical investments are less tied to specific contracts than horizontal investments, and the return on the investment is long term. However, vertical investments provide direct capability in one of the three areas of the capacity to succeed—get work, do work, and get paid.

Decisions on vertical investments are the most difficult to make. They require the highest level of belief in the future, clarity of what's necessary to reach objectives, and access to financial resources to make the investment. In addition, they demand that owners wait on the return. Examples of vertical investments include:

- hiring an experienced manager to handle financials,
- building a sales organization,
- engaging in a rebranding initiative,
- attaining new corporate professional designations (LEED, ISO, etc.), or
- buying new estimating software.

Each of these investments has the potential to take a business to the next level in one of the three areas of the capacity to succeed. However, they also exact the cost long before they create a return, and the return is much less direct and definable.

As an example, we worked with a firm in Ohio that engaged a consultant to help its people conduct a formal strategic planning process. What was that planning worth to them the day they finished it? Not much. But what's the value of clarity? Of establishing meaningful key metrics and getting all resources focused on the same objectives? How much is it worth to confidently say no to some opportunities so the business is more able to say yes to the right opportunities?

For this firm, it meant revenue was slightly down the first full year after the planning was complete, but profits soared three times higher after the planning. Fewer sales and more profit? Sales grew again the next two years and, most important, profit remained strong. Yes, the vertical investment in a good consultant to objectively lead them through a planning process became an investment that kept on giving.

One of the cohort groups of entrepreneurs we worked with over the last five years included an IT firm that had a good product offering but an ongoing problem of 30 percent employee turnover. It was obvious the employee turnover was hurting customer satisfaction and the firm's ability to deliver consistent service. But the business owner didn't realize it was also costing the company a great deal of money. Even conservative estimates suggest turnover can cost 1.5 times an employee's annual compensation, which means an employee who makes $50,000 a year costs $75,000 to replace. And this firm was losing *five* people a year.

So the business owners made the vertical investment to move from a human resources approach to a talent management approach to hiring. The change meant they had to hire someone with the experience and knowledge to make the change happen.

In addition, they had to invest in better systems and create a better structure for the way they hire, evaluate, develop, and even compensate employees. It cost thousands of dollars in software and systems plus months of personnel time to establish the new processes. What did they get in return? In the first year, their employee turnover dropped from 30 percent to 10 percent. Their customer satisfaction increased, which led to an increase in customer retention. But the 10 percent increase in profit surprised the business owners the most.

The costs of turnover are often difficult for business owners to see. They would have to determine the cost associated with others doing the work of those who left, the cost of on-boarding each new person, the cost of the time it takes each of them to become a productive employee, plus the ultimate cost of losing customers.

> **Employee turnover – the silent business killer.**

This is why we call employee turnover the silent business killer—and also why this type of vertical investment is so difficult to justify. In this company's case, the return was significant and lasting, and even more important, the vertical investment moved this IT firm up in its capacity to succeed.

The key message is: *Building the capacity to succeed takes investment.* Horizontal investments are important and they matter and they make a difference. But a firm can make horizontal investments forever and never reach a point of sustainability without relying on minority programs.

In contrast, vertical investments create the type of capacity that leads to sustainability and long-term prosperity. Building the capacity to succeed—getting to quadrant four—involves a blend of both horizontal and vertical investments based on a predetermined plan for growth and tied to clear expectations of returns. Business strategy and planning make the "right" investments more clear. And having clarity makes investing easier for the business owner.

CHAPTER 7

Talent is a Key Investment

As noted in the previous chapter, the capacity to succeed requires investments in a business's capability to get work, do work, and get paid—all of which depends on doing work well. Thus, businesses can't develop the capacity to succeed without internal talent.

In fact, all business investments are enabled (or disabled) by investments in talent. All businesses are judged by the talent they have, but talent is even more important to minority firms than others. Why is this? As a category, minority businesses already have a perception deficit. The level of a minority firm's talent either confirms the low expectations or catapults the minority firm forward because, in the minds of some, it's the exception to the rule.

Minority firms also have a tighter margin for error than other firms. It's partially because of those negative perceptions but also because of internal resistance within major corporations to minority programs. Either way, every mistake becomes magnified and, again, is used to confirm the original concerns and negative perceptions of reluctant parties. I'm not sure if that means people are hoping minority businesses will fail, but it does give some the opportunity to say, "I told you they couldn't do it."

The biggest reason talent is so important, though, applies to all businesses. It's increasingly tough to differentiate a business based on the products or services it provides. Businesses claim to be faster, cheaper, and stronger. Most businesses, and an even greater percentage of minority businesses, are *execution businesses*, which means there is generally nothing unique about the product or service they provide. These businesses win or lose in the marketplace based on how well they *execute* the core components of business. Execution is all about talent, with some experts suggesting as much as 80 percent of a business's execution is driven by the talent of its people.

If you don't think talent is important, just follow the money. The "war" for talented people is why corporations spend so much to find the best and invest more to make that talent even better. Talent affects everything—the brand, perception of the business in the marketplace, its efficiency—everything.

Case in Point: Our COO

I have lived this scenario many times, but one of my best examples is when our firm, TriVersity Construction, hired a Chief Operating Officer (COO). When he joined our firm, we were in the midst of a difficult project that was over budget and behind schedule, and our customer was two steps beyond upset. In fact, the customer had instructed an attorney to inform us of this in writing—an ugly situation poised to get even uglier.

Our new COO joined the effort to see if he could do anything about it. He was quickly able to "see" everyone's needs and concerns. He not only knew what to do, he knew how to do it because he had done it many times before. In fewer than two weeks, he had won the customer's trust. We went on to finish the project with the customer as our partner in making the best of what was a bad situation. The customer's experience with us finishing the project redeemed our reputation with its people. Our COO didn't do it alone, but we couldn't have done it without his level of talent.

Was the investment in this level of talent worth it? That answer is easy for me. Of course we avoided legal fees and rework expenses, but most important, we saved ourselves from a tarnished reputation. *Talent matters.*

Strong, talented performers get a lot done and at a high level of quality. They make better judgment calls, present fewer management headaches, and have lower turnover than most employees.

> Talent is one of the areas in which paying more actually costs less.

Talent is one of the areas in which paying more actually costs less because the right talented people add exceptional value.

Potential versus Performance

Some people make it their mission to hire employees others won't hire—to provide an opportunity to those who have potential but haven't been given a shot. I love the idea of this mission, and we practice it in our companies, too—but not in every role and not every time. For some roles, we don't have time for a person's potential to become performance so we find people who have "been there and done that" successfully.

A few years back, we were working with a cohort group of 20 minority business owners in a multi-year capacity-building initiative. I asked members of the group if they hired the best talent. They all hesitated for a moment and then generally answered yes. As we drilled down on how they knew they hired the best, together we discovered they actually didn't. In effect, they hired the best they thought they could afford, although they didn't know what the best talent actually cost. They also hired the best they could find but looked only in their own circles, and they tended to pick people they liked rather than basing the decision on evidence the person could excel in the job. Our discovery went on and on, poking holes in their assertions of hiring the best.

Knowing what "the best" looks like can be difficult. The practical approach is to first aim to simply hire *better* than what the business had before and better than the competitors. The activity of continually getting better leads to having the best.

Here are the basic principles to consider for hiring top talent:

1. The smaller your company is, the more important each hire is because each one represents a higher percentage of your total number of people.

2. The more you need a particular function and the more a role relies on experience, judgment, and credibility, the more you need to hire based on what the person has already proven he or she can do, not perceived potential.

3. Every job needs a job description, and you must have clarity around what the business needs. Without this clarity, you can talk yourself into hiring based on how you feel about the person. Not good.

4. Hire slowly and fire quickly. I've had it backward for years. Everyone I know pays big time for getting this wrong. A 2009 study conducted by the Hackett Group,

human resources experts, suggests that a bad hire could cost 10 times the person's salary.

5. "Not bad" does not equal "as good as" and is certainly not "the best." The best a "not bad" person can be is mediocre.

Talent touches everything. The minority business system focuses a lot on helping firms with other factors, such as how to gain access, provide educational opportunities, build strong business strategies, and address financial needs, but it neglects talent. I'm guilty, too, and no doubt those factors are important to the growth of the capacity to succeed. But the investment in talent trumps them all. Give business owners *everything* they need for success and, without the talent to implement well, they don't have much at all.

The next four chapters discuss each of the three areas of the capacity to succeed. As you read about each area in more detail, reflect on the type of investments—both vertical and horizontal—required to move a business up in capacity. And note how talent enables each investment.

*Every business needs
a plan for getting work—
an approach based on
the business's specific needs.*

CHAPTER 8

Get Work – Proving Your Business Has Value

The Capacity to Succeed

Figure 8.1. The First Element – Get Work

Nothing begins in business until something gets sold, so you have to be able to get your own work. Some people don't agree because they don't like to sell. I get it, but know that if you don't sell, you can't succeed. No matter how well a business can *do work*, it won't matter if the business can't *get work*. Getting more and more people to buy what the business sells is *the* major test of whether a business has a sustainable business proposition. A business is always selling. It must sell the people from whom it needs support, partners with whom it needs to work, and ultimately, customers who need the value the business offers. And for most businesses, selling is not easy.

Most Products and Services Aren't Special, So Your Sales Effort Better Be

The majority of businesses can be categorized as execution businesses and this especially true of firms owned by minorities. Execution businesses are those who's product or service itself doesn't stand out as anything special or unique. Think of businesses such as assembly, light manufacturing, printing, distribution, engineering, staffing firms, and construction. *How* the business executes is the only thing that makes the business special, and selling any differentiation is difficult.

These aren't bad businesses by any means, but they're highly competitive. So what's the key to success for them? To *out-execute* the competition. And a good place to start is in how you go about pursuing customers. One aspect of the execution of getting work involves *art* and another *science*.

THE ART OF THE VALUE PROPOSITION

The art of getting more business starts with the clarity and relevance of a company's value proposition. As most businesses are providing a product or service already being offered by others, why would customers change vendors to buy the same thing from you? What quality or characteristic about *what* you do, *how* you do it, with *whom* you do it, and *where* you do it makes your proposition special enough to lure customers to change?

Carl Satterwhite, the CEO of RCF Group, a workspace solution company (TheRCFGroup.com), would ask, "What's your more?" What *more* do you offer than the current supplier? Minority status used to be enough to at least give you a shot. Remember set-asides? Now minority certification can at best get you a conversation, but you'd better have something *more* to say—and that can be difficult.

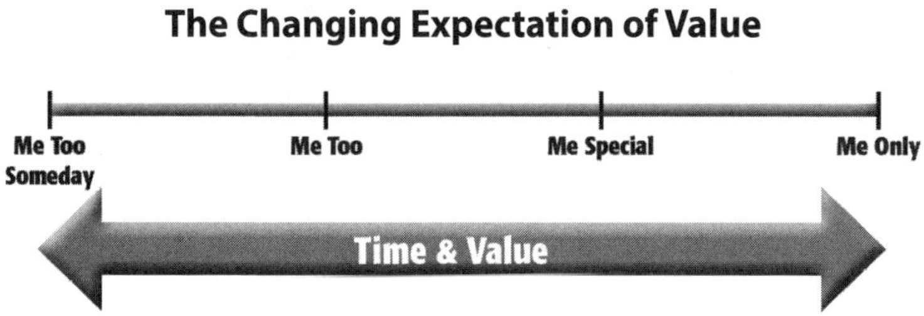

The Changing Expectation of Value

Figure 8.2. The Minority Business Continuum of Historical Value

Figure 8.2 depicts how attitudes and expectations have changed in the minority business industry. At one time, the thought was, "Give me a chance and I'll be as good as my competitors someday." Look for *Me Too Someday* on the graphic. We built programs, activities, and metrics around this idea. Somewhere along the way, the minority business community realized a need to *already* be more capable—to be as good as the competition. It was critical to be able to say *Me Too.* But over the last decade, *Me Too* wasn't good enough because mitigating risk became the new commodity. Being as good as a bigger competitor meant the competitor was still better because, when size was considered, the competitor presented less risk.

Expectations have continued to evolve. Today, sustainable minority firms (and their attitude toward the market) are focused on continual efforts to be *Me Special*. That means successful firms create special value for certain customers and under specific conditions. They don't do it for every customer in every situation, nor is there an expectation they can sustain *Me Special* status forever. The world is a hyper-competitive place; no advantage lasts forever.

Few execution firms ever arrive at *Me Only*, but reaching this extreme end of the continuum is not the point. Rather, the point is that *Me Too Someday* is gone and *Me Too* is no longer enough. The attitude of pursuing *Me Special* and even *Me Only* creates the dynamic required to create a powerful value proposition. That's a valuable asset—one that's both difficult to create and important to protect.

THE SCIENCE OF SELLING MORE WORK

When we talk to minority business owners, we rarely hear enough about their systems, processes, or tools to secure new customers. Most business owners are more interested in talking about how well they execute on contracts than how they can *systematically* go about *getting* new contracts.

> If one characteristic distinguishes the highly successful minority firms from those relegated to the toughest grind, it's the ability to sell their own work.

If one characteristic distinguishes the highly successful minority firms from those relegated to the toughest grind, it's the ability to sell their own work. Too many minority firms get business by "working with" one or two majority partners who "invite" the minority firm to participate on a contract won by the majority firm.

The other common scenario involves minority firms that got their start with one or two customers because of their capability to execute well on the work to be done. However, years later, these firms still have only one or two customers because they haven't invested in the systems needed to execute the science of getting new ones (or they don't have a sellable value proposition).

The minority business system sometimes unintentionally lures minority firms down this path. Here's how it goes: Major buying organizations are committed to spending with minority firms so they find one that can execute well on contracts with them. The major buying organization provides increasing opportunities for the minority firm to compete for more contracts. Based on its confidence in and relationship with the minority firm, it may even invite the firm to enter business areas different from what it historically supplied. Technically, this means the minority firm can get more work.

But this capability is different from being able to consistently identify viable new customers, establish credibility, work through a sales cycle, and close new business. Of course the firm wants to do more business with existing customers, but this existing growing relationship doesn't replace having the capability to also seek and secure new customers.

Every business needs a plan for getting work—an approach based on the business's specific needs. Businesses that sell best have these characteristics in common:

1. **Selling is continuous.** Great businesses sell their products or services both when they *need* business and when they *have* business.

2. **Everyone sells.** Everyone in the organization has the knowledge, direction, and motivation to see opportunity and pursue it.

3. **Selling has its own process.** Great businesses have a process for selling the same as they do for creating a product or performing a service. A selling process might include answers to questions such as:

   - How do we as a business define our prospects?

   - How do we make initial contact, move the prospect along the selling cycle, and measure our progress toward closing a deal?

   - What are our specific activities that create opportunities (sales calls, networking, relationship building)?

   - How do we measure the effectiveness of our selling activities?

   - What are our goals and metrics around the selling effort?

   - What resources do we need?

   - What accountabilities do we assign?

Getting work includes an element of science, which requires a defined, disciplined process, but it also includes an element of art—that is, defining your own value proposition. The next chapter addresses the *art* of getting work.

CHAPTER 9

Enabling Your Value Proposition

A firm's value proposition lies at the core of its ability to get work, and minority firms face a unique challenge in this arena. Although the minority business system provides access, it has also created a generally negative perception of minority firms.

Mastering the Capability to Get Work

The challenge of having a generally negative perception has developed over time. Decision makers in major buying organizations may have been exposed to hundreds of minority businesses, and an overwhelming number of them have not been a fit. Add these realities to the fact that everyone is busier today than ever. As a result, the environment for selling a value proposition is, at best, a challenge. Buying organizations don't have time to listen and even when they do they often don't believe what they are hearing.

But successful minority firms have overcome this and mastered the capability to get work. Following are three consistent ways these firms protect their value proposition—and you can, too.

Know your value-creating place in the supplier chain. The firms with the most success know their businesses best. I know; this seems so obvious, you may wonder why I mention it and even list it first. Well, because many business owners don't seem to understand it. The perception about a minority business opportunity still attracts people into businesses in which they have no particular insight. I'm not saying leaders should never enter a business in which they have little experience. Consider that IBM was turned around by Lou Gerstner, a guy who had previously led RJR Nabisco. Making cookies and manufacturing computers are clearly different businesses. So the idea isn't necessarily that a business owner needs to be an expert in his or her industry. Rather, it's about needing to have a business perspective in general—such as understanding where the particular business fits, how it can win, why its value proposition works, and for whom it works.

Be careful not to prove them right. Poll after poll delivers the same result. When asked to describe minority businesses, people respond in negative terms: too small, low quality, undercapitalized, lack capacity. Don't prove them right! It's not wise for a business to take on tasks it can't perform, agree to deals that can't make it money, and fail to follow up or follow through. Minority firms, even more than others, need to state what they *can* do and nothing more—then do it well, on time, as ordered, and with enthusiasm. It's not fair to judge individual minority businesses based on the general perception—but people do. Some even look for bad minority businesses to confirm what they already think.

The evaluation starts when a minority business tries to sell its product or service: How clear is the firm's approach? How believable is its value proposition? Where does its business lie on the continuum of value? How strong is its follow up? These questions may seem basic and potentially condescending, but

minority businesses can move closer to *Me Special* simply by
not being what people think minority businesses are.

Participate with strategic intent. The minority business
industry has institutionalized the idea of having minorities
participate as a minor partner in major contract opportunities. In fact, this has become the business model for many
minority companies. However, participating with a majority
supplier as a minority partner can be either a means to an
end or a dead end. Here's an example. My company, TriVersity
Construction (TriVc.com), was considering acquiring a specialty construction company to accelerate growth. Knowing
that few minority firms come on the market, we were excited
that the company was owned by a minority entrepreneur, and
one who'd grown it from scratch. We were also attracted by
the company's size and geographic location. However, as we
reviewed the business, it became painfully clear it was simply
a *participator*, not a sustainable presence, in the construction
industry. The business had three customers and played only a
support role. The final blow came
when we realized it had no capability to get its own work. Instead,
the company counted on major
suppliers to "invite" it to participate. We didn't buy the business.

> Participating with
> a majority supplier
> as a minority part-
> ner can be either
> a means to an end
> or a dead end.

Being a participator is a good
thing—until it becomes a business's *main* thing. Participating in
contracts is a means to an end, not the end itself. Even if a minority business owner likes the participation model, what the
owner of this specialty construction company we considered
buying had done for the previous 20 years would be difficult

for firms to repeat today. Having minorities participate on projects benefits the buying organization because it gets to count the spend. It also benefits the majority company because it gets to meet the request of its customer for inclusion. However, the minority business only wins if it's a *better business* when the opportunity to participate is over. For example, did it acquire a new process it can use later on its own? Was it able to use the money made from participating to invest in resources such as new technology? Did it make a strategic talent hire that makes the firm stronger? These "wins" all qualify as vertical investments.

To be honest, participation scares me. Yes, we do it, but I'm still afraid of it. Why? It's too easy to become distracted and slip into a pattern that excludes making the tough decisions to invest in the resources that allow us to get our own work. Being invited to participate is not the same as selling the work; and receiving money is not the same as creating sustainable value.

Also, when a business is participating, of course the lead firm wants the minority business's best talent. But then how can a business expect to win its own work when its best talent is tied up with someone else's opportunities? Once again, a business isn't sustainable unless it can get its own work. The participation model threatens that ability.

Make Your Value Proposition Real

What your business sells constitutes your value proposition, but that's built on value the business can actually create. The value proposition needs to be clear, but it also has to be real. If you say your value proposition is that you drive down cost for the customer, you have to be able to drive down cost for the customer. So be honest with yourself or find someone who can be honest with you about the value you bring. Know your gaps and get serious about filling them. Minority businesses face an exceptionally difficult path because of the negative perception of their category. Although you can't do much about that right away, you need to understand the reality you face.

If you think you can find a way around selling, think again. You can't. And selling is not a "sometime" activity if you want a sustainable business. Don't get into the trap of selling only when you need work and not selling when you have work.

Figure 9.1 lists what a firm needs to have and do to attract work on its own.

A business has the capability to get work when:

1. It has a clear value proposition and it can articulate the value it adds.

2. The science of sales is ingrained in the business.

3. It can simultaneously respond to additional opportunities with existing customers and pursue opportunities with new customers.

4. The business can sell while it executes on contracts, and execute on contracts while it pursues new opportunities

---

Figure 9.1. The Capabilities of a Firm That Can Get Work

Remember, a business is not sustainable until it can *seek and secure its own new customers*. Getting work demands both an element of science (using a defined, disciplined process) and an element of art (enabling and protecting the firm's value proposition). *With the exception of talent, nothing is more important to the health and future of a business than the capability to attract new customers and thus get more work.*

The capability to get more work is tied inextricably to the capability to perform that work well once it's secured. Chapter 10 addresses this second aspect of the capacity to succeed.

CHAPTER 10

Do Work – Delivering the Value

The Capacity to Succeed

Figure 10.1. The Second Element – Do Work

Everyone loves to win contracts—but then you have to do the work. Delivering the product or service is a fulfillment of the promise and, more important, where the value is created for the customer. Typically, when we talk about capacity, we focus on the capacity to deliver the product or provide the service. But capacity in this sense is much more than *what* or *how much* a business can do. In fact, three elements make up the total capability to do work: (1) what a business can do, (2) how much the business can do, and (3) how the customer experiences the work. Sustainable businesses realize the vital importance of the third element. Let's look at each element in more detail.

The Three Elements of Doing the Work

What a business can do. The primary question here is this: Can a business do what it says it can do? The tangible output/delivery needs to match the expectations of the customer. Most businesses these days *can* produce the product or provide the service they say they can, which is why people repeatedly give minority firms additional chances, even if they don't meet expectations in some other areas. "They do good work. I just need them to _____." (Fill in the blank.) Remnants of old thinking remain on both sides of the purchasing equation regarding two levels of quality—one for non-minority suppliers and another for minority suppliers. But the informed mind knows that no major buying organization can afford weak links in its supply chain.

> Businesses that struggle with quality find that competitive forces tend to drive up their quality or drive them out of business.

Minority or not, suppliers who provide poor quality or even lower quality than others are an endangered species. No one even talks about quality much because it's so important it's assumed. Businesses that struggle with quality find that competitive forces tend to drive up their quality or drive them out of business. What a business can do is critical, but it's the bare minimum expectation in the "do work" area of the capacity to succeed.

How much work a business can do. Customers say they want "scale." They want a supplier with the personnel, processes, equipment, supply chain relationships, and financial strength to service their needs. The idea of "how much a business can do" is the heart of the historical conversation about capacity. As previously mentioned, in the customer's eyes, bigger is generally considered better (or at least safer).

Big buyers *like* big suppliers because they help limit the number of suppliers in the supply chain, and big suppliers often provide economies of scale that help drive down cost. In addition, big suppliers tend to have more experience and more highly developed processes than small businesses. Because of these advantages, firms with more scale also present less risk. Like everyone else, minority suppliers have to be "big enough." How big is that? The answer is relative to the customer; it means big enough for the customer to believe that the firm's size adds to its solution (or at least doesn't diminish its value).

I talk with business owners all the time who tell me they don't want to own a big business. I'm not sure if they say that because they fear they can't handle a big business, or if they truly don't want one. Either way, I honor what they say. So is there opportunity for small minority businesses to do business with major buying organizations? Well, nothing is absolute. For business owners who want to stay small, the short answer is to *find a value proposition* on which they can build a competitive business and for which size doesn't matter.

Occasionally, a smaller minority firm that's proven it can perform may even get an opportunity to fulfill a contract for an execution business in which size is usually seen as important. It would be wise to see these opportunities as stepping stones to growing scale, not just a resting place for managing that contract. These opportunities are increasingly rare and dangerously difficult to duplicate. Big customers generally want big suppliers. Thus, if a supplier *wants* (remember what that means) to do business with big customers (the primary participants in the minority business development system), it's likely the business owner will have to *want* to grow the business.

The minority business community has been talking about growing capacity for years, and contrary to some current thinking, minority suppliers are more ready to face this challenge than ever before. Size is *not* the only thing that matters, but it does matter. If the ability of a supplier to do a higher volume of work is important to the customer, then minority suppliers are advised to use every avenue necessary to deliver the size needed. They can partner, create joint ventures, acquire other companies, or form strategic alliances—whatever it takes to become bigger.

When customers are looking for a supplier with *capacity*, they often focus on how much work the supplier can do. But once they engage with a supplier, the capacity they need most is in how they *experience* the supplier.

How the customer experiences the work. This aspect of "do work" is often the root cause of what customers claim is a lack of capacity. Remember, customers have options. The difference between the options isn't typically found in the product or service; it's often found in the many "customer touches" throughout the experience of being served by a supplier. These touches might relate to account management, responsiveness, communication, and other such elements leading to a general ease and thus preference for doing business with one supplier over another. Joan Fox (Joanfox.com), customer experience expert, says, "It is possible for a customer to get served, meaning they get the outcome from the product or service they purchased, yet still not feel served because of everything that went on during the process." These subtle but significant differences don't necessarily make a good supplier a poor performer, but they can render a good supplier replaceable when another option presents itself.

> In an increasingly competitive world, the customer experience remains one of the few areas in which a business can distinguish itself.

Capacity-building firms invest in these points of customer interaction. Many businesses choose to focus solely on the product, timely delivery, and price. All of those are important, but they're also a given. Most suppliers can do the same. In an increasingly competitive world, the customer experience remains one of the few areas in which a business can distinguish itself. Though important for all businesses, this effort can be a potential game changer for minority firms.

Balancing How You Do Work

The capability to do the work is critical to the overall capacity to succeed. That involves a combination of what a business can do, how much work the business can handle, and how the customer experiences the work. Together, these deliver on the promise to the customer and make money for the supplier. Firms with leaders who understand the balance of these three elements also understand where to make both horizontal and vertical investments. These investments propel the firm's success.

Rather than be discouraged by the market demands in this area of doing work, it's possible for minority firms that want to build a sustainable and prosperous organization to be inspired. Once they know the rules of the game in our current business environment, they have the guidelines for making plans, establishing relationships, and investing as needed to succeed.

CHAPTER 11

Get Paid – Making the Business Able and the Owner Willing

The Capacity to Succeed – The capacity you really want!

Figure 11.1. The Third Element – Get Paid

When I hear "it's not about the money," I immediately think "it *must* be about the money." And it should be. Profit isn't only how you keep score; it makes a business viable and the business owner willing to continue to compete. *Profits feed the business.*

A business must make profits and make them in line with its industry peers. Why? First, profits can be reinvested in the business in the form of equipment, key personnel, tools, research and development, and enhanced processes. Obviously, a business limits its ability to invest in these resources if it doesn't make money. And if it can't make both horizontal and vertical investments, it will struggle to grow the capacity to succeed.

> **Making money in business isn't optional; it's imperative.**

Second, profit goes to the business owner in the form of returns. Why would owners risk doing business without the return of profit? Profit compensates the owners for the delayed gratification and tremendous effort they put forth. The return must be at a level that justifies the risk they're taking or they have no rational reason to continue. There's nothing wrong with making money and even expecting to make money. Furthermore, there's nothing wrong with building wealth. I agree it's not about *what you do* with the money; certainly you can give it all away. But making money in business isn't optional; it's imperative.

Some business owners are "called" into business to fulfill a social mission. For example, they may want to empower single mothers or provide opportunities to former offenders who need a chance at a better life. I appreciate the value these well-meaning companies bring, and I caution these business owners not to miss the point. Their businesses still have to make money. A company earns the right to fulfill its mission by how well it executes the business as measured by profits. Making money doesn't necessarily result in spending money on new cars and big homes. Rather, it provides the opportunity for that business to sustain its presence and support the livelihood of many more people.

I suggest the capacity to succeed is a closed-loop system of sorts. You get work, do work, and get paid so you can get more work, do more work, and get paid more. If you've done your part well on the first two, then you've earned the right to get paid. But having any expectation to get paid without building capability to do so is futile.

Obtaining New Opportunities is Great, but . . .

Businesses can concentrate so much on getting work that they lose focus on getting paid. Therefore, the goal isn't only to get contracts; it's to make money from the contracts you get. Of course, price matters to every customer, and intense competition makes the focus on price even greater. Customers have options, and they want the best price. How do you balance getting work with getting paid? Consider these ideas.

Choose work that provides value for which customers are willing to pay. Some work is worth paying well for and some isn't. In an effort to find a niche, minority business owners sometimes choose work that has limited value. A frequent example is a business that subcontracts to a minority supplier that can more efficiently and profitably do that same work itself.

We worked with an architectural firm that had fallen into this situation. This firm was a minority partner with a larger architectural firm that used them when clients wanted to see minority participation on their projects. The minority firm provided what used to be called drafting services and is now frequently called production services. Production services are the commodity level work of producing the drawings, which are needed on a project but are seen as bringing minimum value. The larger firm also had the capacity to do the production services itself, so why would it pay another firm to do it? Minority spend. But the larger firm would not pay much more than what it actually cost to perform the services for two reasons. First, because they could do the same work in-house at minimum cost because they have existing staff. Second, because they don't value the expertise in the work. That didn't mean the minority business wasn't good; it just meant the large architectural firm (the minority firm's customer) didn't consider the work to be any more valuable than what it would have cost had they done it themselves. This may sound reasonable on the surface, but think about it. The minority supplier is now in a customer/supplier relationship based on something other than value, i.e., minority spend. The problem for the minority firm? Production services generate a minimal profit margin because supporting production is seen as low-value, low-expertise commodity work. The minority firm could only profit from performing production services if it were also doing the higher-end architectural planning elements.

This firm got stuck. It couldn't grow because it couldn't get paid... enough. This demonstrates how non-value-based relationships are difficult to sustain and not likely to produce a sufficient profitability.

Price the product or service to both win business and create profit. Businesses are advised to know their cost and build a price in excess of this cost. We've found that even some large businesses don't know their internal costs and, worse yet, they think they do. What's the danger here? A business grows by gaining additional contracts, but growth often causes strains on cash flow. The business leaders blame the poor cash flow on the growth, only to discover later they have a cost structure that exceeds what they can charge the customer.

I've seen firms, even those with considerable size, operate on the edge of insolvency all of the time. They then have to take dangerous actions, which increase their cost structure even more. For example, they pay their suppliers late to improve their cash flow. In turn, their suppliers charge them late fees and quote them higher prices to make up for delays in payment. They max out their lines of credit and struggle to obtain more because they can't show strong profit margins. The worse part, potentially, is that firms in this position can't stop operations because they owe so many people (banks, suppliers, landlords, etc.)—all because they didn't study their costs and set their prices to allow for enough profit.

Continually find ways to drive down internal cost. Due to competition, businesses always experience downward pressure on their pricing, so they must constantly drive down internal cost to continue to have a profit. They use many methods to accomplish this, including finding innovative approaches to deliver the product or service and improving relationships with suppliers. For example, suppliers give better pricing (and service) to customers who order high volumes and pay as agreed. Depending on how much you use external suppliers, these relationships can be critical to maintaining low internal cost.

Stay true to the firm's ability to do work. A business has to be somewhat flexible to meet customer needs, but it must draw a line. It can't abandon its core ability to perform without deep consideration. For example, if your business model suggests you need two technicians in a truck to make an effective service call, don't agree too quickly to send a truck with only one technician. Yes, it appears to reduce internal cost, but it could also make each call take twice as long, deliver too little value, or increase your business risk.

Make sure the business has its financial act together. Certain core capabilities are key to the idea of *getting paid*. They include a solid accounting system and processes but involve much more than that. Here's a sample "checklist" of what it means to have your financial act together. The company:

- can produce accurate monthly financials.
- has accurate cost data for both the products and services it provides.
- understands industry-standard profit margins.
- has tools and processes for pricing or bidding opportunities.
- produces accurate and timely invoices.
- understands payment terms and the cost to carry the accounts receivables.
- has competitive pricing and payment terms with suppliers.
- has an established and healthy banking relationship.
- has a business model proven to make money.

Although even more detail and more capabilities are required, you can use this checklist as a basic guide.

Know the Gaps and Fill Them In

Some might argue it's unfair to expect minority businesses to come to the table with such an infrastructure in place. However, the capacity to succeed includes the capability to get paid, and that relies on establishing the basic elements in the checklist. Many of the items listed involve making vertical investments, while others simply demand new thinking. It's unrealistic to believe a firm can go directly from not having these capabilities to having them all, because that takes a lot of doing. However, these items aren't optional; they make up the bare minimums for businesses that expect to grow and prosper.

Business owners know how their businesses stack up regarding the capabilities listed, and they need to be working on making progress. Major buying organizations will be asking for and expecting to see these capabilities grow, and support organizations will help minority businesses in growing these specific capabilities.

The basic truth is this: If a business ever hopes to grow the capacity to succeed, it must make a profit.

*Don't let ego
or stereotypes about
minority businesses drive
your investment decisions.*

CHAPTER 12

How Can Businesses Prioritize Their Investments?

Building the capacity to succeed starts with an understanding of what a business *has* compared to what it *needs*. The gap between these two provides a road map to the investments that will matter most to a business's ability to sustain itself and prosper. However, because every business is so different, it's virtually impossible to provide a specific prescription for which investments to make when.

How to Think About Investments

That said, the following points show ways you can organize your thinking about investments, especially the vertical kind. Using the model of get work, do work, and get paid as a guide, ask the following question: *What does my business need internally to have the capability to get more work, do that work, and make market-rate profits as an outcome?* You can use the following order to prioritize your investments:

1. **Focus on investments that improve profit first** (e.g., investments that streamline operations, lower internal costs to do work, and allow you to raise your price). Make these investments a priority for two practical reasons. First, the additional profit will enable you to make

even more important investments. Second, the sooner you begin to obtain higher profits, the longer those higher profits have to accumulate, and the more robust the financial returns will be over time.

2. **Invest in proven talent**, especially in the areas of the business that demand judgment based on experience. The smaller the organization, the more important each hire will be. Potential is good, but a track record of proven performance is better.

3. **Invest in business assets that make you less dependent on others** for the elements that control how well you keep your value promise to the customer. For example, quality, timeliness, cost savings, and innovation vary greatly from one business to another. A sustainable business must have the areas impacting the customer experience under its control.

4. **Invest in processes and systems that attract and retain top talent.** Investing in proven talent is only a part of the equation. You also have to offer the benefits top employees expect. Therefore, invest in whatever you need to put the organization on par with the industry, such as healthcare plans, retirement plans, education, etc. You needn't over-invest; still, being able to compete for talent is critical.

5. **Invest in non-essential items last.** If something doesn't get you work, improve your ability to do work, or produce more profits, then it can likely wait.

Don't let ego or stereotypes about minority businesses drive your investment decisions. If you're thinking about making a particular investment because it makes you feel better or because you want to avoid looking like a "front company," that investment likely doesn't matter to the business. These would be investments such as buying a building when leasing space is a better financial decision, acquiring new

> First satisfy what your company needs to be successful, not what you would like to have.

company vehicles because it makes you look successful, or even sponsoring community events when your budget doesn't support it.

In short, first satisfy what your company *needs* to be successful, not what you would *like* to have. Then, you may find you can satisfy the latter, too.

When people want
something to be different,
they often have to change.

PART IV

When It's Time for Action

*...not everyone
is prepared to grow
a business...*

CHAPTER 13

Time for Action? Start with the Business Owner

I used to believe anyone, no matter who they were, could figure out how to start and grow a business if they got the right training, the appropriate support, and the access to opportunity. I was right, and I was also wrong. I still maintain that anyone can grow a successful business of some type. I now realize, however, that not everyone is prepared to grow a business of the type that can successfully service major buying organizations and develop the capacity to succeed.

I think the minority business industry inappropriately invests a lot of time in businesses that appear to have promise but are owned by business owners who actually don't.

If support organizations and major buying organizations want to contribute to the growth and development of firms with the capacity to succeed, they need to start with the business owner. A set of personal intangibles specific to minority business owners will either contribute to or inhibit the owner's business as it seeks to grow and prosper. The intangibles are not only difficult to define but are also the most difficult to develop of all business-related elements. Deeply embedded in a person's mindset, these intangibles have been cemented through their experiences over time. I call them the *four corners of intangibles* because, together, they either provide or erode a leader's platform for success.

When it's time for action, business owners have to embrace these four intangibles. Support organizations have to find ways to support them and major buying organizations have to come to appreciate how these intangibles translate into the type of competitive suppliers they want. Figure 13.1 displays the intangibles of greatest importance to minority entrepreneurs.

Four Corners of Intangibles for Business Owners

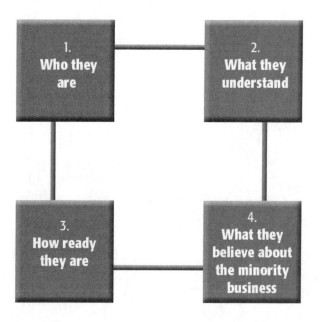

Figure 13.1. The Four Corners of Intangibles

The Four Corners of Intangibles Explained

Corner One: Who they are as a person. This includes intangibles such as reputation, presence, interpersonal skills, and overall likability. Some people are seen as too self-serving or too manipulative. They might talk too much or not enough. Part of this assessment is perception and part is reality; some elements are deserved and some are not. People shouldn't judge books by their covers, but the truth is they often do. Of the four corners, shortcomings in this one are the most difficult to overcome.

My advice to entrepreneurs? Remember that people must *want you to win.* You don't have to "suck up" to anyone, but it helps to be the kind of person others want to work with and like. "Who" you are as a person does matter.

Corner Two: What they "understand" about their business. What business owners *understand* about their business (their business model, industry, market, etc.) is quite different from what they *know* about their business (the product or service). Many people who know how to do what the business does still don't understand how the business fits in to the market and how it creates value.

Business owners need to be able to recognize opportunity. Many can't because either they lack the experience, the vision, or both. To build the capacity to succeed, owners need to understand how the three capabilities (get work, do work, get paid) function for *their* business. Otherwise they can only be reactive to what comes along and not proactive to the opportunities that lead to sustainable success.

Problem: It's difficult for business owners to get their understanding of the business from someone else. Yet people try it

> **What business owners "understand" about their business is critical.**

all the time. They ask someone else to *feed* them advice on what their business should be. Consequently, they end up repeatedly trying new approaches based on the latest suggestion they got from the various people who keep trying to help them. Understanding can come from many places including previous industry experience, study of trends and directions in the industry, and applicable insight from other industries. What business owners "understand" about their business is critical.

Corner Three: How ready they are for entrepreneurship. Many personal attributes impact entrepreneurial readiness, including:

- the ability to deal with ambiguity and uncertainty,
- a healthy balance between patience and persistence,
- the ability to add one's own structure and discipline,
- a desire to learn new things, and
- the ability to work in new ways.

Business owners also need new skills because they'll have to grow into the CEO role of their business as it expands. Whether they spent years as a corporate executive or found their success as an expert in a specific area, they all have a gap to fill in their entrepreneurial readiness. Business owners often limit their success because they don't ready themselves for entrepreneurship.

Corner Four: What they believe about the minority business system. How minority business owners think about the market power of being identified as a minority business is critical because the implications show up everywhere. Their mindset affects who business owners hire, how they invest, what they expect, how they sell, how they partner, and how they position their firm. For a minority business owner, the minority business system is best thought of as a vehicle for providing access to opportunities otherwise out of reach.

Sure, other benefits are occasionally available, but the core benefit is *access*. Minority entrepreneurs expecting more from the system won't focus on what they need to grow the capacity to succeed.

How minority business owners feel about the magnitude of the impact of the minority business system on their business reveals a sliding scale. Some people think it means everything, while others are naïve enough to believe it has no impact at all. The truth lies somewhere in between, while the reality shifts depending on what's going on at the time.

This fourth corner comes down to one idea. Is the business owner trying to build a *minority* business or a *sustainable* business? When talking to a minority who owns a professional services business, I asked about her experience working with a local minority business development organization. "They aren't doing *anything* for me," she said in a frustrated tone of voice. "They claim they have access and they can get me a meeting, but I haven't gotten any business from it," she complained.

"What do you need them to do?" I asked her.

Her response was serious: "Get me more business."

I understood what she was saying, but it wasn't rational. *No one* can get her more business. Supporting organizations can create access and help create an environment to improve the results of minority firms in general—but that's about it.

The best minority entrepreneurs have found a way to leverage minority business programs to overcome historical and present-day obstacles and build a business without overly relying on those programs. Owners with too little involvement in the minority business process miss the access opportunity that minority programs can provide. Conversely, owners who rely too much on minority programs may expect (and even wait for) more support than the system can provide.

Don't Be Too Quick to Judge

Although it's easy to judge business owners, remember, it's not about where they *are* but where they're *going*. Understand it takes time, expertise, and investment to build an infrastructure of success. Often, business owners fall short in all of these areas.

So ask these questions to determine if owners have the essential core elements they need:

- Are they learning?
- Are they growing as a business owner?
- Are they building the support of others along the way?
- Are they looking for a minority business opportunity or a business opportunity?

If the answers are right, they'll likely figure out how to build a business with the capacity to succeed.

CHAPTER 14

For Minority Business Owners Who Want to Build Capacity

The capacity to succeed merely represents an idea *until* a business owner decides to build it into the business. The firms we've seen prosper—as well as the successful models of today—all embrace these three important capabilities: Get work. Do work. Get paid.

However, business owners approach it in different ways in different types of businesses, with varying personal objectives. The key is *seeing the value and wanting to grow capacity* in the process of building a lasting, market-competitive enterprise.

Still, it's all talk until the leader does something. Even though major buying organizations and various types of support organizations play enabling roles, only the business owner can access that potential. The evidence is clear: The business owner needs to act as the driver because outside forces can't create capacity-building businesses in spite of unwilling owners.

So if you're a willing business owner, what do you do right now? Begin with these steps:

1. **Determine what you want.** Not what you'd like to have or what you've been programmed to say you

want. What does the phase "what you want" mean? It's *what you're willing to delay gratification for, put your finances at risk to have, and work night and day to get.*

2. **Create a business vision based on what you want.** Be clear about what you're building, and be careful about basing your vision on old models of minority business success. The world has changed, and older models may not work today.

3. **Build a business strategy.** Strategy is the foundation for everything else. The whirlwind of day-to-day operations will derail any business that doesn't have a clear strategy. Answer the following questions to build your strategy:

   - What is the business trying to accomplish?
   - What is the value the business creates?
   - Who are the target customers?
   - How will the business access its customers?
   - What are the internal assets?
   - What are the projected growth thresholds?
   - What is the timing?
   - Who are the needed partners?
   - Who are the competitors?
   - What are the critical activities?
   - What are the primary metrics of success?

   If you need help, ask for it. Better yet, *assume* you need help. Seek input from various support organizations that can enable your business's growth in capacity.

4. Create a capacity plan. Start by understanding what you have and compare it to what you need to support your strategy and build the capacity to succeed. Construct a plan to overcome whatever gaps exist. Determine the finances to execute on the plan. You can fill gaps in a number of ways. For example, you can buy the fix, borrow it, build it, partner for it, or joint venture to get it. Whatever the method, put all your planned actions on a schedule with clear milestones. Some gap fillers will be temporary until you build the capability internally. Others may be fixed and ingrained in your business model. The bottom line is, if you *decide* and *intend* to build capacity, you need a plan and a schedule to actualize your intentions.

> Understand what you have and compare it to what you need to support your strategy and build the capacity to succeed.

Global Lead, a management consulting company, provides a perfect example. After years in business, the partners of the firm got clear about what they wanted. They recognized the need for investment capital, so they had to build a business that would drive the interest of equity investors. They attracted Goldman Sachs Urban Investment Group, knowing they needed Goldman's help to compete globally and create the value that comes from its competitive position.

Leaders of firms like Global Lead often focus on developing their intellectual property, their use of technology, and their ability to effectively serve customers in different parts of the globe. With the support from Goldman, they were able to acquire a number of small consulting firms and merge with one of their largest competitors. What happened? They landed the combined firm (renamed Global Novations) on the *Inc. Magazine* list of fastest-growing companies. The partners at Global Lead ultimately sold to Korn/Ferry International, a leader in talent management solutions.

Nothing is perfect, and I'm confident the partners at Global Lead would say the journey wasn't easy. However, when they got clear about what they wanted and began working their plan to get there, they achieved what they set out to do.

Yes, it's quite a journey to grow the capacity to succeed. Business owners aren't alone on the trip, but they *are* in the driver's seat. What they *want* establishes the direction; *how much* they want it sets the pace.

CHAPTER 15

For Major Buying Organizations Who Want to See Capacity Built

Those who spend the money have the power, and major buying organizations drive minority business development with their spending habits. The market will respond to the customers' desires—if they demand it. So if major buyers want capacity to grow in minority businesses, they'll have to make that desire clearly known. Of course, it will require change.

When people want something to be different, they often have to change—change their thinking, their behavior, and even their expectations. Sometimes they may even have to take what may seem like a step backward.

I'm not naïve. I realize some of what I'm proposing may hurt spend goal performance in the short term. It may also frustrate minority business owners and advocacy groups that hold to the social promise of these programs. However, the principles in *The Capacity to Succeed*—and the actions needed to make them work—will put the minority business system on a sustainable course. This course demands that supplier diversity professionals gain knowledge in new areas, focus on different activities, and, yes, change their long-held beliefs about the role of minority business development.

If major buying organizations *want* a naturally occurring base of diverse suppliers with the capacity to meet their needs, I suggest they consider the following actions to enable the changes needed.

They can continue to . . .
- enhance corporate metrics that support capacity building and not only spending goals.
- see the size but recognize the capacity to succeed. A single contract or a non-capacity-building joint venture can make a business sizable, but the same businesses may have no capacity to succeed. Size matters, but buying organizations need to recognize how well a firm is creating the capacity to make itself competitive and sustainable. It will take more effort to evaluate this, but the outcomes are transformational.
- give it time but not too much. Buyers must keep expectations high and hold people accountable for investing in building capacity.

They can stop . . .
- rewarding models that don't create capacity. A great example is the proliferation of joint ventures that don't create capacity in the minority firm; their only value is reaching spending goals.

They can start to . . .
- set expectations for what it means to grow capacity, becoming clear about the indicators of success and looking for firms with a business model that would still thrive if minority programs went away.

- see their resources (time, travel, and dollars) as investments and expect a return, evaluating every request for time or energy through the lens of this question: "Will this activity lead to more capacity to succeed?"

- spend time with suppliers that are building capacity and support organizations that are enabling it.

- recognize growth in capacity and reward it. Buying professionals can educate themselves and their suppliers on what capacity growth means and set clear expectations about their desire to see capacity grow.

- ask about progress in the key areas of the capacity to succeed. Then, most important, they can introduce new opportunities to the firms doing the best in the marketplace at growing their capacity.

The capacity to succeed can be built, but it will be more difficult if major buying organizations don't signal a serious change in what they want. It will prove to be a difficult move for minority firms as long as the minority business system rewards business formations and contractual awards in which the only market value is

> There's a difference between a business with large revenues and one that is building capacity.

the accomplishment of a spend goal. *If buying organizations want to work with firms that have the capacity to succeed, they need to spend dollars with those that are building the capacity to succeed.* There's a difference between a business with large revenues and one that is building capacity, and each buyer has to make that distinction. Buyers will get more of what they demonstrate they value.

HOW CAN YOU EVALUATE
MINORITY/MAJORITY PARTNERSHIPS?

There's been a lot of talk about growing capacity through creating minority/majority business relationships. Are they really a capacity-building tool or simply a means to reaching spend goals? The answer: It depends. I included this discussion in this section of the book because major buying organizations have the most influence over how these relationships form and how they develop.

I refer to minority/majority combined businesses as *m&m combos*. These m&m combos can take a number of forms, including strategic alliances, joint ventures, and ownership (when majority firms actually own a portion of the minority firm). The constraints and opportunities are generally the same for all of these structures.

A frequent question I hear from professionals in major buying organizations is this: How can we tell if these m&m combo relationships are built in a way that's likely to grow minority capacity? Some suggest relying on the minority business certification process to answer this question. The certification process is critically important; yet confirming ownership and some level of control is the most the certification process can do.

What certification cannot reveal is *intent*. That is, what does the entity formed by these minority and majority business relationships *intend* to do? Does it intend to leverage special programs and grow the capacity to succeed of the minority member? Or does it intend only to reap an advantage by helping the customer reach a spend goal while keeping all of the value and capacity in the majority partner?

There are no specific attributes or elements that can completely reveal what these m&m combos intend to do—nor can you totally predict their probability of success. However, you can ask certain questions and review particular areas, and the accumulated information will either make you feel confident with the combo's *intent* or it won't. It's difficult to determine intent until you examine how the entity is actually doing business.

Here are seven aspects of the m&m combo relationship to consider.

1. Does the minority firm have a role that contributes significant value? The role must be truly valuable and not merely judged by the often-used standard "commercially useful." Could the minority owner build a business on the value the firm creates for the m&m combo? Could the minority firm sell the same services to others?

2. Is the m&m combo model built for growth and sustainability? Could this be a viable solution if it were not a minority-led partnership? Note: This question is different from asking whether they would do the combo deal if it weren't minority-spend driven. Some minority/majority deals

wouldn't be considered by either of the parties if it weren't for the interest in minority spending by major buying organizations. That's the power of the spend goal. Done right, though, combos motivated by spend goals can be credible capacity-building opportunities.

3. Does the minority firm have uniqueness apart from the majority company? Does it do something the majority company does not? Does it do something better (cheaper, faster, etc.)? Does it serve a different market segment or set of clients? Again, none of these questions are absolute deal makers or breakers. However, it's much easier to create a sustainable business relationship if the two firms are not trying to do the same things in the market.

4. How is money spent and for what? Take time to track a dollar of revenue through the combined business arrangement. How does each dollar get spent in the business and for what value? Does a significant portion go to pay the minority partner for the value it brings to the business? Or do all of the dollars go to the majority company because it is "handling" all of the significantly valuable parts of the solution?

5. Do the parties have plans beyond this opportunity? Relationships are difficult to manage. Trust is built over time. Capacity-building m&m combos tend to have plans beyond the one contract, project, or opportunity that may have brought them together. Indeed, the plans must go beyond

vague talk. What commitments have the combo members made to each other? For example, they could commit to pursue all government contracts as a combo, or they could agree to pass all leads below a particular dollar threshold to the minority partner. Look for evidence that the two parties share a commitment to leverage their relationship so both of them can grow.

6. Are they willing to set milestones for the minority firm to transition into adding higher value and playing more significant roles? At times, the barriers to entry into a particular industry or the customer's risk might drive an m&m combo to initially rely on the majority organization to handle the most significant elements of a solution. These relationships can still be a tremendous opportunity to grow capacity. In these situations, it takes at least three elements to ensure capacity is built in the minority firm. They are:

   • First, both companies must be willing. The minority firm has to be willing to make investments, take on additional risk, and also take on more control. It has to want to grow the capacity to succeed. The majority company, on the other hand, has to be willing to *give up* some control—the portion of the profit associated with the value that will now be delivered by the minority firm. What's the payoff? The minority company will add value, be compensated for that value, and build its capacity to succeed. The majority firm gets a partner who can share the risk and help its leaders gain access to more opportunities. Plus, major buying organizations get the type of competitive supplier they need to reach their business objectives.

- Second, the m&m combo must have a specific plan to transition some roles (not necessarily all roles) from the majority firm to the minority firm. What roles? By what date? By what means? The more specific the plan, the easier it will be to hold the two parties accountable.

- Third and most important, the customer has to be willing to hold the m&m combo accountable for meeting the stated milestones.

7. Be wary of a 51-49 percent ownership structure (the 51 percent being that of the minority firm). This ownership structure (or something close to a 50-50 split) is standard, and technically there's nothing wrong with it. In fact, it passes minority certification criteria for ownership. But this narrow ownership margin creates other potential problems and, I warn you, explaining the problems can get confusing.

- First, 51-49 percent ownership gives the minority owner no flexibility to sell any of his or her ownership in the business without giving up personal control. For example, if the minority owner wants to sell even as little as two percent of his or her interest to a key employee, that owner will lose majority shareholder status. The issue is even more difficult if the key employee is not a minority because, in this example, the company would then have only 49 percent (51 minus 2) owned by minorities and could no longer be certified as a minority business.

• Second, ownership percentage typically contributes more of the overall return to the minority owner than it does to the non-minority owner. Here's why. The non-minority owner is likely getting a significant amount of each dollar that comes into the business because the dollar is tied directly to the amount and value of the work being done to provide the solution (as noted in point number six above). The non-minority owner makes money on all of that activity plus he or she gets almost half (49 percent) of the net profit. Bottom line: The non-minority partner likely makes significantly more money with his or her 49 percent ownership than the minority owner does with 51 percent. This dynamic makes it more difficult for the minority owner to generate the kind of financial returns needed to invest in building the capacity to succeed.

• A third reason I don't advise 51-49 percent relationships is they look bad! They send one indication of *intent*. Although there's nothing illegal or immoral about them, equity is crucial to a business owner—and arguably even more so in m&m combos.

It's important to make all parties' ownership interest enough to keep them invested and interested. But what's the right split? I can't tell you. Start with 75 percent minority/25 percent majority ownership and negotiate from there. Show the non-minority firm how it stands to profit in addition to the ownership percentage.

Nothing can *guarantee* that an m&m combo will drive the development of capacity in the minority company. However, much can be done to set up the right dynamics. Those dynamics include the interest of the minority business owner as well as the openness of majority companies in these types of business relationships. Still, nothing is more important than the *demanded desire* of the customer. These m&m combos will create the capacity to succeed in minority firms if the customer sincerely wants *capacity* to be the outcome of these minority/majority relationships.

Today, m&m combos are a growing part of how spend goals are met. They can also become a significant part of how a company's capacity to succeed is built.

CHAPTER 16

For Support Organizations – Creating the Environment for Success

S ome business owners will figure out how to build capacity with little assistance, but others will need support. The owners may have what it takes in general but may lack the necessary networks, experience, environment, or exposure. Who can play a pivotal role in these situations? Minority business programs operated by chambers of commerce, the Minority Business Development Agency, Urban Leagues, and a host of others.

To be effective in facilitating the development of businesses, minority business support organizations have to create an environment conducive for firms on a path to building the capacity to succeed.

Most of the support organizations are focused on businesses and business owners who are not on a path to build the capacity needed to sustain a supplier relationship with major buyers. This sounds worse than it actually is. In reality, most businesses in this country stay small. Ninety-six to ninety-eight percent of all U.S. businesses generate less than $1 million in sales yearly. Plus, consider the basic axiom of entrepreneurship: *Many people try and few succeed.*

With minority business development, the situation becomes more complicated. Funding sources want support organizations to work with large numbers of businesses. No matter how much they say they want outcomes, funders really want quantity.

As a result, support organizations needing funding create programs that work with significant numbers of minority businesses. They run general programs such as training workshops and networking events and sometimes provide coaching. However, they spend most of the coaching hours on the businesses that need them the most, not on those with the highest likelihood of growing the capacity to succeed. Meanwhile a smaller number of high-potential businesses don't get the kind of quality support they could use to become sustainable and prosperous businesses.

We estimate 80 percent of all minority support organizations are programmatically focused on businesses that aren't designed or don't aspire to grow a firm of the scale to serve major buyers. Almost no community in the country has a support infrastructure for the minority business owners with the most promise of becoming significant suppliers to major buyers. However, every community does have a set of minority business owners who possess the basics of what they need to grow and prosper.

> Every community has a set of minority business owners who possess the basics of what they need to grow and prosper.

What distinguishes these owners? They understand their business, they have a level of entrepreneurial readiness, they know what they really want, and they realize that being a minority is not their competitive advantage. They will be able to grow their business *because* they have their act together. However, without the right support, their business growth will most likely stall well before it reaches its true potential.

All successful businesses, large and small, are valuable. Yet we want to find a way to *invest more than we are right now in the minority businesses with the potential to scale.* These businesses have the true potential to create value for major customers, significant numbers of jobs for their community, and generational wealth for their owners. They're the ones that benefit most from a well-crafted minority support approach.

Effective Approach for Support Organizations

My colleagues and I at the Institute for Entrepreneurial Thinking (EntreThinking.com) spent years in research, observation, and review to determine an effective approach to helping business owners increase the capacity of their businesses. We worked with over 100 business owners in "capacity-building programs" over a five-year period, employing a number of different approaches and evaluating the effectiveness of each. Through observation, interactions, and the use of a number of quantitative metrics, we tracked the changes in the participating businesses. Given our evaluation, the following elements worked and we offer them to support organizations as a guide.

1. **Establish a cohort group.** Groups of 15-20 business owners who get together regularly and participate in similar activities will create an important bond. Cohort groups provide support and also create a healthy competition. No one wants to have the business that's NOT growing or be the one business owner arriving unprepared for meetings. The entrepreneurs will want

to report good things in their businesses, and therefore they'll work to make those good things happen.

2. **Engage the right business owners.** I hope that point is clear by now. Nothing happens without engaged and enabled business owners. You want the business owners who have demonstrated they are committed. Those business owners show the basic capability to grow to scale. Plus, if the *wrong* people participate, the *right* people won't want to.

3. **Set high expectations.** Support organizations can consider the support they provide to participating businesses as an investment, not something they're giving away. When people or organizations make an investment, they expect both returns and respect for the investment. So they need to set high expectations early and stand by them. High expectations start with criteria for participation in the program. We suggest organizations be selective. Minimum expectations need to include personal engagement by the owner, not a surrogate. Participating firms must have and regularly share the company's basic financial statements. We found that businesses without financials are unlikely to grow capacity.

4. **Add accountability.** "Stuff happens" even when we have the best intentions. Business owners on the path to building the capacity to succeed can easily get distracted. The day-to-day grind can involve business owners in activities that are urgent but not strategically important. Most of us could use a bit of accountability support, and business owners are no different. It helps to add an accountability factor to remind, encourage, and if need be, spur business owners into working on the items they

say they need to create the success they want. There are many ways to add elements of accountability. You can have participants report to the group about their activities or ask for regular progress updates on committed plans to develop the business. We have even used an accountability coach to meet with participants regularly to increase the likelihood participants would fulfill the business development task they said they would.

5. **Build ongoing awareness.** Some people call this education, but it's broader than that. Even 45 to 60 minutes discussing a common business concept can lead to dramatic results. Topics might include: defining components of a good strategy, understanding mergers and acquisitions, selling to a particular market segment, addressing human resource matters, or attracting the best talent. The exact topics aren't as important as the quality of the sessions and the steady diet of new ideas. Exposure to the concepts and ideas is key because these topics become seeds for capacity-building business owners to work into their plans for growth.

6. **Keep important metrics.** Because the objective is to grow capacity, business support organizations need to capture data early and often. They also need to *expect* to see capacity grow. Those involved are therefore asked to report items such as sales, profit (gross and net), number of employees, investments in capital assets, and any additions to their management team. Understandably, business owners don't like to share this information. However, those in support organizations can't *invest* in a business if they don't know how it's doing. Thus the process needs to be as easy as possible on the business owners. Support organizations can:

- request information from standard business documents the owners will likely already have.
- ask for information regularly but not too frequently (when in doubt, quarterly).
- *not* ask for information that's merely interesting but not important to gauging whether a firm is growing in capacity.

7. **Stay at it long enough.** Our experience suggests it takes a minimum of 18 months to show even early evidence of capacity building in a business. Organizations are advised not to even *start* if they can't commit to a program with the same participants for at least two years—and three to four years is best. Any shorter timeframe not only wastes time but can be a disinvestment for the business owner. Participating entrepreneurs are investing in this process, too, and they're investing their most precious resource—time. They literally can't afford to invest without a return.

People see the *science* presented above, and they tend to immediately want to rearrange the necessities to fit their own limitations. They might say, "Well, we don't have to set such high expectations, but we can do the other things."

Of course, you can mess with the criteria. You can add people to the group, run a program for six months instead of three years, make your whole program education based, and not ask for any financial data. *But you won't get growth in capacity.*

This is science, folks! Not the only science, but until I see other approaches that actually work, I'm sticking with this one. I recommend you do the same if you want to realize the results you want.

PART V

Fulfilling the Promise of Minority Business Development

The biggest
challenge was admitting
that our old approach
had a limited upside.

CHAPTER 17

The Promise Evolves

Shuffling the three sheets of paper in front of her on the podium, the woman introducing the panelists looked up at the audience. "Welcome to the Minority Business Summit's Paragon Panel Discussion—*Paragon* meaning the perfect example of a specific quality. Today, we're profiling an example of a significant breakthrough in minority business development. We'll hear from three panelists about their seven-year journey together. The foundation of their success stories consists of how they developed what they call *the capacity to succeed.*

"Our panel includes entrepreneur John Wyatt of Fulton Drive Team, Carol Street, Director of Supplier Diversity for Republic, and Max Albert of the Accelerator, a minority business support organization. The panelists will present their individual perspectives on what's happened over the last seven years. They've each been transforming their own thinking, expectations, and day-to-day activities and that of their organization. So one by one, they will share their thoughts on where their organization was seven years ago, what they did differently to change their outcomes, and where they are today."

Removing her reading glasses, the facilitator smiled as she scanned the crowd of nearly 200 business people. "Ladies and gentlemen, please help me welcome to the stage John Wyatt, Carol Street, and Max Albert."

The audience applauded as Max, Carol, and John walked to the stage. While Carol and Max seated themselves in two of the three high-backed leather chairs, John turned on the microphone clipped to his belt and walked to center stage.

"They've asked me to go first, and it's my pleasure," said John with a friendly smile to his companions and then the audience. "The first question is, where was I and how was my business doing seven years ago? The answer is easy. We were a successful 'minority' business," John said, making quotation marks in the air. "We were a solidly performing supplier with a few loyal, long-standing clients. Although we knew how to execute on contracts, we were challenged to get new clients and had begun struggling to sustain our profit margins. Worst of all, we didn't understand what had changed.

"I remember when the answer first hit me. The three of us," John said as he turned to look at Carol and Max, "were conversing with my business role model, Stu Bails. He's retired now, but at the time, he was a well-respected minority business owner. Stu was trying to explain that the success he had realized wasn't possible for me. He talked about how the business world had changed—how much more sophisticated the procurement process had become and how global markets had changed the game. He made it clear my path to success would have to be significantly different from his.

"Honestly, I didn't get it at first, but when I finally did, I could see that all was not well. Stu introduced us to a concept called *the capacity to succeed*," said John, holding up the book Stu had shown them that first day.

"This was the answer," he continued. "It explained why we were struggling and laid out a new pathway to success. My company had all of the standard issues: too dependent on our minority status, a value proposition that wasn't clear, and limited strategic business intent.

"In addition, our challenges were creating other problems. For example, our low profit margins made it difficult for us to make important business investments in people, technology, and growth. When we stepped back from our business and looked at it objectively, we didn't like what we saw.

"What made us change? Well, we asked ourselves, 'Could we get customers if no one cared about minority business?' Frankly, we knew the answer was no. I'm still amazed how many minorities are lying to themselves about the answer to that question."

John looked at Max, who nodded his agreement.

Turning back to the audience, John echoed the question he saw in their faces. "What did we do about where we were? First, we had to agree we were committed to changing our current position. It seemed we had no choice. We realized we couldn't make it if the minority programs went away, and we were already seeing signs the programs weren't working for us like they used to. We had to commit to change—or agree to slowly and painfully go out of business.

> We had to commit to change or agree to slowly and painfully go out of business.

"Second, we had to become clear on what we wanted. Although we hadn't decided we wanted to someday sell the business, we knew we wanted a business that a savvy investor would want to buy. If we built a business someone wanted to buy, that would mean it was delivering sustainable customer value."

John paused to look at people throughout the audience for signs of comprehension. Apparently satisfied, he continued, picking up the pace.

"We made a lot of changes in our approach to business—too many for me to describe right now. However, I can tell you that all of the changes came from our focus on one driving question: 'What would we need to do to build the business we wanted *if we were not a minority firm?*' This may seem like an obvious question to you—maybe you already run your business that way—but we didn't." By now, John was walking back and forth while looking at different segments of the audience. He wanted to get this point across powerfully.

"The fact of being a minority business had become central to almost everything: how we sold, who we partnered with, how our customers viewed us, even the people we hired. As we began to focus on the capacity to succeed, we narrowed our focus to the areas in which we were uniquely qualified to add value. Our revenue actually declined by twenty percent, but our profit margin improved considerably. We also became obsessed with mastering the ability to sell new customers.

"Our outcomes? We now have a clear value proposition and a sales engine that's among the best in our industry. The combination of those two outcomes has allowed us to do three things: one, diversify our customer base; two, raise our value in the eyes of the customer, and three, drive industry-average profit margin.

"And here's the frosting on the cake," added John, smiling broadly. "I'm proud to say that three weeks ago, we sold our company to PWL Global, the largest logistics organization in North America."

The crowd clapped enthusiastically. John thanked them, then he looked over at Carol to see if she was ready to come forward.

Carol picked up her glass of water from the table by her chair and moved to behind the podium. Laying out a few sheets of paper, she then looked up at the audience and began.

"Thank you all for giving us this opportunity to tell our story. I'm pleased to say Republic had a world-class supplier diversity program when we started on this particular journey. We were already doing a lot of things right—and now I'd like to share with you our new level of engagement and expectation." She glanced down at the papers in front of her.

"As I said," she continued, "our program was world class based on all the supplier diversity benchmarks. We had a significant spend goal as well as senior executive support and supplier diversity goals distributed throughout the organization. In fact, we regularly won local, regional, and national supplier diversity awards—and, as most of you know, we're members of the Supplier Diversity Leadership Circle. This is a group of the twenty-one companies considered the best in supplier diversity."

Carol paused to take a sip of water. Looking briefly over at John, she continued.

"John already mentioned our eye-opening conversation with Stu Bails. We became convinced Stu had figured out the next step for supplier diversity and minority business development. Out of that conversation and many more discussions within Republic came several difficult questions. We realized we had to become clear about what we wanted as outcomes of our supplier diversity efforts. Was our focus on diverse spending truly improving anything? Were we championing firms that would one day no longer need supplier diversity programs? Or were we advancing firms solely created to meet our diversity spending goals?

"Of course, we were helping diverse businesses grow, but truthfully, we hadn't challenged our thinking in decades. This concept of *the capacity to succeed* gave us a framework to address situations that had been sources of frustration for years."

As John had done earlier, Carol surveyed the audience. Noting apparent curiosity and attention, she resumed. "We decided it was in our best interest to focus on firms that are building capacity. So we developed a plan to look for, promote, and support firms focused on that. We asked different questions and set new expectations, becoming clearer ourselves about what we wanted. As you heard, John's business is an example of the outcomes. People we talk to about this always want to know exactly what we did and how we did it. My response is to read the book and follow the path." She held up *The Capacity to Succeed*, which John had left on the podium.

Carol smiled at the crowd. "We were already good at supporting supplier diversity. So what were the core lessons of this journey for us? Two things: First, *how* we spend matters more than *how much* we spend. Our spending is a catalyst for opportunity for minority firms, and we learned to spend in a way that gives incentive to the outcomes we say we want.

"Second, we rediscovered the fact that we are the customer. We can receive from the supply chain what we demand.

Just as we demand cost savings and quality standards, we demand working with diverse firms that are building the capacity to succeed.

"Thank you for your time," she concluded. "I would be happy to answer any questions at the end."

As the audience applauded, Carol walked to her seat, giving the nod to Max Albert.

After waiting for the applause to quiet down, Max took the podium. "It's truly a remarkable story. One of the best corporations in supplier diversity became even more effective in driving the creation of sustainable, growing, and prosperous diverse firms." Smiling broadly, Max added, "And having a business someone else is willing to purchase from you is the ultimate measure of whether the business has created sustainable value—which John's firm has clearly proven.

"That said . . . Hello! I'm Max Albert. I run The Accelerator. Our mission is to accelerate the growth of minority businesses." Max took a few steps and moved out from behind the podium.

"For years, we in the minority business development community thought if we could get major buyers to buy more from minority owned businesses, those firms would grow and prosper. We created a climate of expectation around spending goals and proved the theory—to a degree. More spending with minority firms *did* indeed drive more minority business success. So what's the problem?

"Well, the metrics and expectations haven't evolved. Over time, people and businesses have found ways to provide solutions for major buying organizations to reach spending goals, but the methods don't always lead to developing fully enabled minority businesses.

"We work with businesses like John's every day. His story illustrates the success that's possible—but obviously, not everyone wants to sell the business to an outside buyer, even for a life-changing amount of money. We have firms that have fully embraced the capacity to succeed and are selling the company to employees. Others are planning to pass the business on to the next generation in the family. No matter what an owner wants from the business, a few consistent realities remain—and some specifically concern today's minority owned firms."

Max pushed a button on the remote control and five bulleted statements appeared on the projection screen. Reading down the screen, he glanced at the audience after each point.

"Number one: The success of any business rests with the entrepreneur. Others can help, but nothing happens without the entrepreneur taking the lead.

"Number two: Minority status is not a business value proposition. At best, it's icing, but it can no longer be the foundation of your business success. Being a minority business still matters, but it matters more *after* you've demonstrated the capacity to succeed than before.

"Number three: Old models of minority business success don't work today. The reason for this reality is difficult to understand and even more difficult to accept. John mentioned it in his comments. The elements that defined successful minority firms in the past have changed, and the path to success also differs.

"Number four: Important and targeted investments matter in building the capacity to succeed.

"And last, but certainly not least, number five: Capacity means more than size. A firm has the capacity to succeed when it can *get* work, *do* work, and *get paid*."

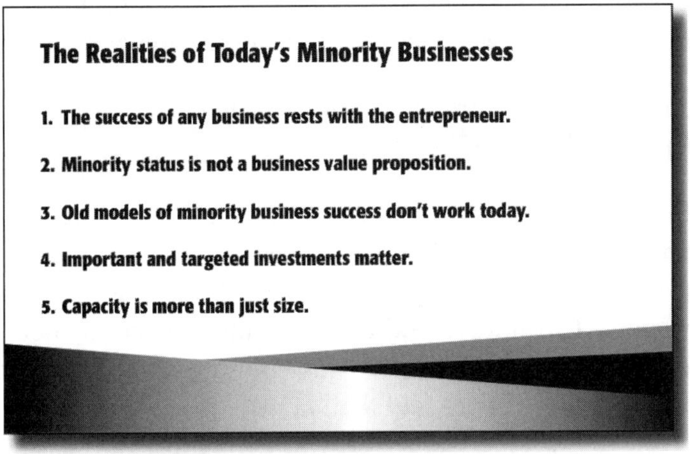

The Realities of Today's Minority Businesses

1. **The success of any business rests with the entrepreneur.**

2. **Minority status is not a business value proposition.**

3. **Old models of minority business success don't work today.**

4. **Important and targeted investments matter.**

5. **Capacity is more than just size.**

Figure 17.1. Five Consistent Realities

Max put the remote back on the podium and turned to the audience. "I don't have a lot to add. John and Carol's experiences illustrate the story well. I'll end with one thought and then join my colleagues in answering specific questions." Max paused, walking toward the front of the stage, then continued.

"I've been in and around minority businesses most of my professional life. The pathway has never been clearer for firms committed to their own success. However, the flip side of the new reality portends that less-committed firms will find fewer and fewer opportunities. This reality will continue playing itself out into the future.

"What's the difference between those owners who are committed and those who are less so? The distinction lies in how fully the firm embraces the idea of *building the capacity to succeed.*

"Thank you."

As the audience applauded, Max rejoined Carol and John in the high-backed leather chairs, and the facilitator initiated the question-and-answer period. The first question was for John.

"John, what was your biggest challenge in changing how you'd been doing business?"

John leaned forward in his chair. "Great question," he replied with a big smile. "The biggest challenge was admitting that our old approach had a limited upside. It meant giving up everything I had understood about business success. Then the second challenge, of course, was committing to *do what it takes* to change. Easier said than done."

Carol chimed in. "The answer to that question is the same for us at Republic. We realized the current minority business system wasn't sustainable, but then we had to commit to doing *something* about it. Tough to change what's been considered the standard for success for more than forty years."

Another audience member raised a hand, then another and another. The questions continued for the next 45 minutes, with the three panelists giving direct and candid answers. Little did they know that Stu Bails had been in the back of the room the whole time listening—and smiling.

Based on what he heard, he felt more confident than ever that the future of minority business was on the right track.

ABOUT THE AUTHOR

Melvin Gravely is president and CEO of TriVersity Construction Company, a full-service commercial builder and one of the largest construction companies headquartered in the Cincinnati region.

Dr. Gravely is also founder of the Institute for Entrepreneurial Thinking, Ltd., a think tank with a mission to improve the results of minority business development activities. He has served as an advisor to communities, business support organizations, major corporations, and minority businesses across the nation.

A popular speaker and noted thought leader in minority business development, Dr. Gravely has written seven books, including the popular four-book fable series: *The Lost Art of Entrepreneurship, When Black and White Make Green, Getting to the Next Level,* and *What Is the Color of Opportunity?*

With a BS in computer science from Mount Union University and an MBA from Kent State University, Mel earned his doctorate in business administration and entrepreneurship from the Union Institute and University.

Dr. Gravely currently lives in Cincinnati with his family.

OTHER BOOKS BY MEL GRAVELY

If you enjoyed this book, you will likely want to read the four-book fable series: *The Lost Art of Entrepreneurship*, *When Black and White Make Green*, *Getting to the Next Level*, and *What Is the Color of Opportunity?*

These four books are all powerful stories full of practical lessons and solid strategies. The reads are quick and entertaining, and the proven approaches create lasting results.

The Lost Art of Entrepreneurship
Rediscovering the Principles That Will
Guarantee Your Success

When Black and White Make Green
The Next Evolution in Business & Race

Getting to the Next Level
Business, Race and Our Common Goal
to Be Competitive

What Is the Color of Opportunity?
New Realities at the Crossroads of
Business and Race